WITNESSING TO JEWS

Practical ways to relate the love of Jesus

D0061992

WITNESSING TO JEWS

Practical ways to relate the love of Jesus

by Moishe and Ceil Rosen

Purple Pomegranate Productions
San Francisco, California

Cover Design by Paige Saunders

99 00 01 10 9 8 7 6 5 4 3 2

Second printing

Rosen, Moishe 1932-
Rosen, Ceil 1932-
Witnessing to Jews—Practical ways to relate the love of Jesus
by Moishe and Ceil Rosen—1st ed.

Library of Congress Cataloging-Publication Data
Witnessing to Jews—Practical ways to relate the love of Jesus

       ISBN: 1-881022-35-8 (pbk.)
       1. Rosen, Moishe, 1932-. 2. Rosen, Ceil, 1932-.
       3. Missions to Jews. 4. Jews for Jesus.
       5. Evangelistic work. 6. Witness bearing.
       7. Christianity and other religions—Judaism.
       8. Jewish Christians.

If you would like more help in witnessing
to your unsaved Jewish friends, contact:

Jews f☆r Jesus
60 Haight Street
San Francisco, CA 94102-5895
E-mail: jfj@jewsforjesus.org
www.jewsforjesus.org

CONTENTS

i

PREFACE

by David Brickner

Jewish evangelism is difficult. Those who choose to obey the Lord and bring the gospel to the Jews will not get much encouragement from anyone but God and just a few people who care.

The sincere Christian faces many perplexing problems, and sharing the love of Jesus with Jewish people can be one of the most bewildering. Many long to tell their Jewish friends about the Savior's love but don't know where to begin. Faced with the opportunity to tell their Jewish friends about Christ, some Christians choose to remain silent for fear of offending them.

Some perplexities will remain a mystery until we see Christ face to face, but witnessing to Jews need not be one of them—as you are about to discover for yourself in this book! As you explore the ways and means of telling your Jewish friends about the love of Jesus, you are in very capable hands.

The author, Moishe Rosen, is a trainer of missionaries. Most of the current missionaries to the Jews in North America were instructed either by Moishe Rosen or by someone he trained. When it comes to methods and materials, Moishe is the foremost expert in the field of Jewish evangelism. Nevertheless, this is not a book for the professional missionary to the Jews. The techniques used by a professional missionary-evangelist are different.

Witnessing to Jews is written for ordinary Christians of ordinary dedication. It delivers the most comprehensive and practical guide available for Christians who love Jesus, love the Jews and long for their Jewish friends to love Jesus, too.

You are holding in your hands the wisdom distilled from decades of personal witnessing to Jews. A Jewish Christian himself, Moishe Rosen has led hundreds, if not thousands, to faith in Christ. As founder of the Jews for Jesus ministry, he is the genius behind one of the most exciting and effective missions to the Jews the world has ever seen.

Moishe Rosen has equipped and inspired an entire generation of evangelists to the Jews. Yet he knows the difference between professional missions strategies and the kind of personal witnessing tips that will help lay people in their everyday encounters. This book concentrates on the day-in and day-out, face-to-face interactions that Christians might have with Jewish people at school, in the office or in the neighborhood.

Moishe combines the practical wisdom of a sage with the pastoral motivation of a minister of the gospel. You will finish this book knowing that YOU CAN DO IT!

It is fitting that Moishe has written this most important publication with his wife, Ceil, who has been editing Moishe's writing for about 25 years. It was through her witness that Moishe came to faith in Christ in 1953. The Rosens have teamed up to produce a book that may well equip an entire new generation with the tools to share the love of Jesus with Jewish people—but not only Jews! If you learn how to witness to Jews, who are so gospel-resistant, you can witness to anyone.

It is my prayer that you are one of countless thousands of Christians who will spend a few hours with Moishe and Ceil Rosen to the end that tens of thousands of Jews—and others—will spend eternity in heaven adoring Jesus Christ, our Lord. Yet even if you alone were to read this book, it would make an everlasting difference if it gave you confidence to sow the gospel seed in at least one heart.

INTRODUCTION

When it comes to forming opinions about Jewish evangelism, some Christians are listening to the wrong Jews. They hear the many articulately spoken protests of the rabbis, but they need to hear from more of us Jews who have found the Messiah and confess the faith. We are grateful for godly men and women who risked our wrath to tell us lovingly about Y'shua.

Changes have been occurring in the field of Jewish evangelism. More Jews than ever have been coming to faith in Christ, and this has caused a reaction in the Jewish community. A spirited and intellectual battle has been raging, and Jews are being thoroughly indoctrinated to resist missionaries. A whole new profession has arisen—that of counter missionaries and counter missionary projects funded by the Jewish community. Evangelically minded churches are regularly denounced and reviled for witnessing to Jews, and the subject has become a matter of great contention. Thus the role of the non-clergy or volunteer witness has become more important than ever.

JEWISH PEOPLE NEED JESUS

If you didn't share our burden and agree with the basic fact that Jews need Jesus in order to be saved, you probably wouldn't be reading this book. Yet in a volume about witnessing to Jews, we must begin by reiterating the spiritual need of the Jewish people. If, as a follower of Christ, you really believe the scriptural injunction that salvation comes only through the blood of Jesus' death and the power of His resurrection, you have no choice but to recognize that Jewish people need to know Him. It's so obvious that it shouldn't need to be stated here. Yet in recent years, some well-meaning but misled Christians have been suggesting otherwise. They claim that Jewish people have a separate covenant with God that exempts them from the New Covenant Jesus brought.

There is absolutely no biblical basis for that assumption! In every point of His teaching, Jesus referred to the Old Covenant—the Law and the words of the prophets. Yet He also said, "I bring to you a new commandment" (John 13:34)—and He was talking directly to the Jewish people of His day.

We believe in the integrity of the Jewish religion as it was revealed in the Old Testament. Nevertheless, without its fulfillment in the New Testament, that religious system is incomplete and inadequate to save anyone.

Every Jew, no matter what he or she believes, is evidence of the existence of God—an indication that the Holy One of Israel is real and that He keeps His word. The preservation of the Jewish people against all the destructive forces that have been unleashed against them throughout history is not merely a sociological phenomenon, it is a modern-day miracle.

However, even though the Jews are evidence of God's faithfulness, this does not mean that every Jew has a knowledge of God and enjoys the grace, love and eternal life that He intended. Many Jews are agnostics as far as religion is concerned. They need the Lord Jesus Christ in order to become completed Jews. If we take the Bible seriously for ourselves, then we must take it seriously for all people, and that includes the Jews. According to John 14:6 and Acts 4:12, there is no salvation outside of Christ for anyone. If that is not true, then none of us should believe in

Jesus. If, however, it is true, then Jewish people need Jesus as much as anyone else! The children of Abraham by birth must become the children of Abraham by faith.

This is not always a comfortable truth, but truth does make demands. It requires us to act when we would rather be silent. Knowing and acting upon the fact that Jews need to receive Christ often brings suffering, rejection and even hardship. We would all rather be accepted and comfortable. Truth is seldom convenient and sometimes painful, but it is always truth.

WHO WILL TELL THE JEWISH PEOPLE WHAT THEY NEED TO KNOW?

The history of what might be termed "modern Jewish evangelism" is only about three hundred years old. The first-century Christians were mostly Jews, as was Jesus. Back then it was Jews telling other Jews about the Messiah they called Y'shua. Then, from apostolic times until the end of the 1700's, once Christianity was brought to the Gentiles, nothing significant along the lines of Jewish evangelism was attempted or accomplished by the Church.

Nevertheless, through the centuries, there have always been Jewish believers in Jesus. In every generation, they have stood as solid witnesses against vocal and sometimes violent opposition from the Jewish community. The roster includes many notables, as well as common people who "heard him gladly" (Mark 12:37). Among the well-known are the great British statesman Benjamin Disraeli, English theologian and writer Alfred Edersheim and the famous German composer Felix Mendelssohn.

Yet the number of born-again Jewish people has been comparatively low. Many more Gentiles accept

Christ as their Savior than do Jewish people. Why the imbalance? To be perfectly honest, one reason is that Jewish evangelism has never been a high priority in the Church.

In Christian circles, books abound on how to witness to Mormons, Jehovah's Witnesses, Muslims, New Agers and followers of almost every conceivable religion under the sun. But what about Jewish evangelism? It would seem that not many Christians have ever considered that Jewish people who do not believe in and follow Y'shua are just as lost as the members of any of those other religions who embrace untruths or half truths.

JEWISH EVANGELISM—GOD'S PRIORITY

Indeed, Jewish evangelism has a God-given priority. Thirty years after the Resurrection, the Apostle Paul wrote to the church at Rome: "For I am not ashamed of the gospel of Christ, for it is the power of God to salvation for everyone who believes, for the Jew first and also for the Greek" (Romans 1:16). "Tribulation and anguish, on every soul of man who does evil, of the Jew first and also of the Greek; but glory, honor, and peace to everyone who works what is good, to the Jew first and also to the Greek. For there is no partiality with God. For as many as have sinned without law will also perish without law, and as many as have sinned in the law will be judged by the law" (Romans 2:9-12).

What does it mean to go to the Jew first? When God became a man, He could have chosen any people, any place, any time. He didn't choose Oslo, Istanbul or Karachi. He chose Bethlehem, close to Jerusalem in the land of Judea. God determined that the gospel should go first to the Jews, the people whom He had prepared as part of His plan of world redemption. Paul's words "To the Jew first" were not merely a history lesson. He was advocating a method and a model.

That priority "To the Jew first" has embarrassed some and confounded others. It does not mean that God in this or any other age gives preference to Jews over Gentiles. It just means that the Jews are God's prepared prophets. Yet they are a nation of missionaries without a mission, a messenger people without a message. They have no message to proclaim until someone wins them to Christ and they find their Jewish destiny of proclaiming Him to the whole world.

God's formula for worldwide evangelism is this: Go to the Jews first. Then the Jews you win to Christ will, with their God-endowed proclivity to preach, be instrumental in winning others. Nevertheless, even if Gentile Christians did not win many or most of the Jews, their method of witnessing would be conditioned by those encounters, and that would result in a more aggressive, less triumphal kind of evangelism. One cannot help but wonder if the church had followed that formula, wouldn't the work of world evangelism be much further along today?

Unfortunately, the scriptural formula of "To the Jew first" is often neglected by the Church for two reasons:

1. The Church has usually preferred to send missionaries to people with whom it could share some worldly benefit as an aid to acceptance. This is good, because it allows us to demonstrate the love of Christ through medical missionaries, agricultural missionaries and missionary teachers. Nevertheless, the Jewish people do not need these things from the Christian Church. The Jews have made significant

contributions to the world in the fields of medicine and science; the average Jew has two and a half more years of education than his or her Gentile counterpart. As far as agriculture is concerned, what has the Church to tell people who have made the desert bloom and have developed an industrialized society with little or no raw materials? The only thing that the Church has that it can give to the Jews is Christ.

2. The Church is discouraged about Jewish evangelism. Satan's lie is that God is through dealing with the Jews, and it is no use trying to witness to them because they are predisposed not to listen. Yet the evidence of the past few years, including the very substantial Jews for Jesus movement which is becoming more and more prevalent throughout the world, speaks to the contrary.

The Scriptures teach, "Even so then, at this present time there is a remnant according to the election of grace" (Romans 11:5). While it is true that in this age Israel as a nation will not believe, there are, and will continue to be, many individual Jews who will hear the gospel and receive it gladly. Nevertheless, the harvest of Jewish souls is not such that it can be cut with a scythe. Rather, in the field of Jewish evangelism, the laborer must extend a Christ-gentled hand to pick the fruit that is ripe for harvest.

Blood-bought believers have a duty to proclaim the gospel to all people, and that includes the Jews. It is not that the Jewish soul is more highly valued than that of the Asian or African or South American, but the Jews are equally in need of salvation. If God's people decline to preach the gospel to the Jews, it must be because they consider either the gospel unworthy of the Jews or the Jews unworthy of the gospel. The first instance comprises a failure to exalt the Lord Jesus Christ as Lord and only Savior for all; the second instance implies a most subtle form of anti-Semitism.

ON AN INDIVIDUAL LEVEL

How many Jewish people have you ever told about the Messiah? Are you afraid to try to witness to Jews? Do you hide behind feeling "unqualified"? Do you ever excuse yourself with, "It's easier for Jewish believers in Jesus to tell unbelieving Jews about Him because they will listen to their fellow Jews"? If so, you may be avoiding an opportunity that God wants to give you.

Jewish believers are not necessarily in a better position than Gentile believers to witness to Jews. If you are a Gentile believer, you may even have an advantage because most Jewish people have been conditioned to discount the testimonies of Jewish believers. At the first Jewish mention of Christ, an automatic battery of defenses kicks in. Whether Jewish unbelievers respond with anger or with politeness, they will usually reason away the testimony of a fellow Jew. On the other hand, they often will listen to Gentiles talk about the Messiah. Statistics show that most Jewish believers first heard the gospel from a Gentile believer.

Do you have a Jewish friend, neighbor or co-worker? Have you ever longed and prayed for that person to know the Messiah as you know Him? Have you ever considered witnessing to that individual? Have you wanted to tell him or her about Jesus, but you didn't know where to begin?

Maybe you've been unsure about whether or not

you ought to say something. (After all, don't Jews already have a perfectly good religion based on the Old Testament?) Possibly you've felt intimidated, afraid you would say the wrong thing and scare that person away from Jesus. Maybe you didn't know whether to refer to Jesus as the Messiah or Y'shua (the Jewish name for Jesus) or the Savior, so you said nothing at all.

In the pages that follow we will present a basic orientation and simple procedures to help you overcome some of the barriers that might discourage you from witnessing to Jewish people you know and encounter. We will show you where to begin and how to go about it. We will examine sensitivities and cultural obstacles, and we will show you how to act effectively upon your God-given burden for people who desperately need to know their Messiah Y'shua.

This book is not a theological treatise or a Bible study. It is a "how to" manual based on the experience of Jews who have been affected by a witness. We hope that after reading it, you will be encouraged to put what you have learned to good use. But if you're still feeling timid, just remember this: most of us who are Jewish believers in Jesus reacted at first to the message of Christ with hostility; yet we praise God for the patience and persistence of those Christians who would not be deterred from sharing Christ with us. As we approach the end of the 20th century, the cause of Christ needs more Christians like them—and hopefully like you—who will not be deterred from bringing God's message to His ancient people.

CHAPTER 1

MYTHS THAT CAN KEEP YOU FROM WITNESSING

You love the Lord. You know from Scripture that God wants you to tell everyone you can about salvation in Jesus, and that includes Jewish people. Yet you approach witnessing with at least some degree of fear and uncertainty. You feel vulnerable and somewhat uncertain.

You fear creating an unpleasant situation—that your Jewish friends will misconstrue your efforts at communicating the Good News as aggression against their religion, and that may destroy your friendship. You are intimidated by the possibility that if the person to whom you witness is not in the "friend" category, it may engender a hostile reaction from a stranger.

Besides feeling vulnerable, you may also fear ineffectiveness: You don't know where or how to begin. You feel awkward and doubt that you can initiate a testimony in a respectable, effective manner. You worry that you can never bring such a witness to its desired end—leading someone to a saving faith commitment.

1

Because of such basic feelings of vulnerability and inadequacy, many Christians find a multitude of reasons to delay witnessing or even not to witness at all. This stockpile of excuses becomes a shelter of myths under which they can retreat any time they feel uneasy about speaking out and want a reason not to do it.

If you are serious about wanting to witness, let's unravel some of those myths:

Myth Number One:

If a person doesn't respond to my witness, it must be because I haven't presented the gospel properly.

People do not naturally give their lives to Christ. They hold on to the reins as long as possible. Therefore, we should expect resistance. Sometimes we can present the gospel in exactly the right way but still have it rejected. Other times we can fumble through our words and forget a Scripture verse or two, yet find that in spite of our mistakes, the person wants to accept Christ as Savior.

There really is no "right" or "wrong" way to present the gospel. Some methods may work better than others, and certainly, doctrinal knowledge helps. Yet God approaches each person as an individual. We must also do this when we witness. What might have been right in witnessing to one person may not be right in witnessing to the next.

Myth Number Two:

It takes a long time for someone to discover the truth of the gospel.

Sometimes it takes a person a long time to come to faith, but usually it doesn't. An individual often realizes his or her need for a savior after taking a personal inventory. This happens because the Holy Spirit has touched that person's heart. Someone else may have planted the gospel seed long before you came along— maybe someone who thought that he or she had failed.

Myth Number Three:
All Jews have a deep, scholarly knowledge of the Old Testament. I feel inadequate in handling the Scriptures. If I am to be effective in evangelism, especially Jewish evangelism, I must know the Bible very well.

Certainly Bible knowledge helps in witnessing, but God doesn't require that you have a certain number of verses memorized before you can witness. If you are faithful in trying, He will direct what you say. In fact, often you will find that you know more than the person to whom you are speaking. Few Jewish people today are well versed in even the Old Testament portion of the Scriptures, and just the basic knowledge that led you to become a Christian probably surpasses what most Jews know about the Bible. In witnessing, you will find that you know more than you thought you did. Furthermore, you will usually end up learning much about Christ as you tell others about Him. The section in this book on how to use the Gospel of John provides enough direction for you to get started.

Myth Number Four:
I am not very good with words. It would be easier and more effective if I just prayed for the person.

You ought to pray. Yet if you want only to pray, how do you explain Romans 10:14: "How then shall they call on Him in whom they have not believed? And how shall they believe in Him of whom they have not heard? And how shall they hear without a preacher?"

How does the Great Commission in Mark 16:15-16 apply to us? "And He said to them [His disciples], 'Go into all the world and preach the gospel to every creature. He who believes and is baptized will be saved; but he who does not believe will be condemned.'"

It is our responsibility to tell others about Jesus whether we speak eloquently or not. Some of the most powerful witnesses make terrible spokespeople. Yet God chooses them.

Myth Number Five:

Instead of witnessing, I can invite people to church. They will hear a sermon on sin and repentance there. After all, it is the pastor's responsibility to be an evangelist.

The pastor may be a good evangelist; however, the Great Commission doesn't call upon us "to go into all the world and invite people to church." It calls upon us to proclaim that Jesus Christ wants to be everyone's Lord and Savior.

The Bible says, "Let the redeemed of the Lord say so." Your personal testimony adds much to your witness. It shows what God can do in a person's life.

Myth Number Six:

The person will probably ask questions that I can't answer. That will prevent me from being a good witness.

No, it won't. Too many Christians fear not knowing all the answers, but remember that only God knows everything! Never be afraid to say, "I don't know" or

"I'm not sure." Just say, "If you're really interested, I will look that up and tell you the next time we talk." The person will respect your honesty.

Myth Number Seven:
Since God knows who will and will not accept Him, it is all predestined. I can't really make a difference.

Some teach that God predetermines salvation; others say He does not. Either way, you should witness. If, indeed, God does predestine a person's eternal destiny, He not only predestines the end, but selects the means by which that person will hear the gospel. If God does not predestine salvation, people must still hear the gospel from someone. You have the privilege of being obedient to the Lord, and perhaps being part of someone's eternal destiny whether or not God predetermined it.

Myth Number Eight:
I should only witness when the Holy Sprit leads me to witness.

He has already led you to witness. Jesus said, "Go into all the world." He said "Go to every creature" (Mark 16:15, cf Matthew 28:19; Luke 24:47; Acts 1:8). So what are you waiting for—a special revelation? Just believe and obey what Jesus has already said in the Bible.

Myth Number Nine:
My testimony is rather dull. I know God loves me and has saved me, but nothing very dramatic has happened in my life. Will anyone really want to have what I have?

Does God not answer prayer? Do you not love Him? Has He not made a difference in how you live? Then should you not be willing to tell others of your love for Him, the prayers He has answered and how real He is? What makes your testimony valid is not necessarily that it is dramatic enough for publication in a book or magazine, but that it comes from your heart.

Myth Number Ten:
I need to wait until I have been a long-time friend of unbelievers in my life before witnessing to them. I will let them see Jesus in me. Then, when they show an interest, I will witness.

We should become friends with unbelievers or at least behave in a friendly, non-threatening manner toward them. However, with what is sometimes called "friendship evangelism," we end up waiting for the other person to initiate a conversation about God, and too often, they never ask. We may well find openings to evangelism when we become friends with unbelievers. However, there is a potential pitfall. Unbelievers may or may not notice a difference in us. They may notice that we don't swear, cheat and lie, and hopefully they will also notice a degree of cheerfulness, compassion and love that they don't see elsewhere. Nevertheless, though they may notice these attributes, it doesn't necessarily mean that they want them or understand them. Even if they do desire something we have, it doesn't mean that they have the nerve to seek it, especially if it means giving up some sin they truly enjoy.

Jewish comedian Sam Levinson was right when he observed, "People don't look for God any more than a hooky-player looks for a truant officer." Most unbelievers don't seek salvation. We must tell them about it. If we don't do that for fear of offending them, they may well end up without Jesus and lost for all eternity!

Myth Number Eleven:
I am responsible for the eternal destiny of the person to whom I am witnessing.

While we might never admit it aloud, subconsciously many of us carry blame and shame. We feel that somehow if we just say the right words, the person will believe. Worse yet, we feel that because we didn't say the right words, didn't witness soon enough or didn't pray hard enough, we have failed. We accept the shame of a person's rejecting Christ and the blame for the possibility of their spending eternity in hell.

We must leave the "blame baggage" at Calvary where the crucifixion heaped all the shame of sin on Y'shua. Yes, we will make mistakes in witnessing. Therefore, even in evangelism, we must learn to accept the forgiveness provided through the Resurrection, where the stain of our sin was removed. Only as we accept this free gift in all areas of our lives can we become effective in showing others how they, too, can obtain forgiveness.

Having dispelled some of these myths, we still must recognize that no procedure, technique or human effort can bring a person to salvation. We merely go and tell others the gospel, but God is the One who convicts and converts the unsaved. Only when His Spirit directs (Zechariah 4:6), can we be sure of the outcome of our witnessing efforts. Then the correct and basic witnessing methods, adapted to our own personality and situation, will bear fruit.

CHAPTER 2

DEFINING BASICS

When we become Christians, we enter into a relationship with the God of Israel—a relationship that came through the Jewish people, through whom God gave the Bible, the prophets and the Messiah. It is our duty, then, to present the claims of Christ to an unbelieving world, and that includes the Jews. Indeed, in Romans 1:16 the Apostle Paul wrote that the gospel of Christ which is the power of God unto salvation is "to the Jew first."

WHAT IS THE GOSPEL?

We use the term gospel in everyday religious jargon as an adjective or a brand name. Without thinking it through, we talk of such things as gospel songs, gospel preachers, gospel believers and gospel bookstores. Yet for those who want to witness, it is important to know exactly what the gospel is before attempting to share it with others. The best definition can be found in the Bible:

Moreover, brethren, I declare to you the gospel which I preached to you. . . that Christ died for our sins according to the Scriptures, and that He was buried, and that He rose again the third day according to the Scriptures. . . . (1 Corinthians 15:1-4)

The term "gospel" is specific. Teaching or preaching may be true and edifying, but it does not contain the gospel unless it clearly presents the facts delineated in

9

1 Corinthians 15:1-4. Those facts are that Christ died for our sins according to the Scriptures, that He was buried and that He rose again the third day according to the Scriptures.

WHO'S WHO?

Much could be said about the divisions of people. The succinct definitions listed here are not intended to cover the field of sociology but are offered for the consideration of witnessing to Jews.

In the context of a scriptural relationship with God, all people fall into one of three categories: Jews, Gentiles and Christians. (1 Corinthians 10:32 describes them as the Jews, the Greeks and the church of God.)

WHO IS A GENTILE?

A Gentile is any non-Jew. The word Gentile is derived from a Latin translation of the Hebrew "Goyim," which means "nations." (Some have mistakenly thought that it is a term of derision, but in Bible usage it only means non-Jews.)

WHO IS A CHRISTIAN?

A Christian is anyone, regardless of birth or previous affiliation, who has entered the new birth through personal acceptance of Jesus Christ as Lord and Savior. A Christian may be a Gentile or a Jew, and neither has more esteem or privilege than the other. However, the distinction remains: just as there are Christian men and Christian women, there are Christian Jews and Christian Gentiles.

In witnessing to anyone, it's important to remember that you will be talking to a specific individual, not necessarily to his or her peers. Thus, do not think in terms of your witness to "the Jews," but to a Jewish person.

WHO IS A JEW?

Ask a non-Jew that question and you're likely to get some rather strange answers. One might respond, "Oh, they're the people who wear little skull caps on their heads when they pray." Another might say, "They're the people who don't eat pork and worship on Saturday instead of Sunday." Another might conclude, "They're the ones who worship in synagogues instead of churches"; or more likely, "They're the ones who don't believe in Jesus."

All those answers are partially true but certainly not conclusive. Catholic popes and bishops wear skull caps. Protestant Seventh Day Adventists worship on Saturday and generally won't eat pork. Some Jews do believe in Jesus.

Ask a Jew that same question, and you may get some equally diverse answers. That's because one of the difficult aspects of defining Jewishness is how people regard themselves. In the old USSR, Jews who were Communists used to say, "My mother and father are Jewish, but I'm not, because I don't believe in the Jewish religion." Yet their internal passports designated their nationality as Jewish. Jewish members of the Communist Party felt a need to deny their Jewishness because the Communist philosophy was basically atheistic, and denial of religion was essential to the Party line. Yet the same Communist government preferred to treat Jewishness as a nationality because it could then exclude Jews from certain activities and positions and treat them as aliens, as though they belonged to another nation.

Because of the lack of a firm definition, much confusion exists. For example, some will say they are "half Jewish" or have "some Jewish blood." Humans are not thoroughbreds like animals. Human identity involves much more than the gene pool contributed by one's ancestors. People are not hybrids. The mule has an identity as a hybrid (i.e., half horse and half donkey). Still it is a mule. However, most mules do not reproduce, and their entire identity depends on physical characteristics derived from the horses and donkeys that produced them. Whatever else Jewishness is, and whatever ingredients go into making Jewishness, it is an identity.

No one can be half Jewish because no one can have half an identity. If people identify themselves as Jews and are identified by others as Jews, they simply are Jewish. If they don't identify as Jews, they are merely people who have some Jewish ancestry. Their Jewishness is in the background and depends on relationships to others. Such people might be sympathetic to the Jewish people, but unless they regard themselves as being Jewish, they are not. However, even if those who are born of two Jewish parents choose to regard themselves as not being Jewish, they are still Jewish by virtue of their parentage.

In other words, certain facts of existence make a person "genetically" Jewish or not Jewish. Those factors entitle individuals with one Jewish parent to be identified as Jewish or, in the case of full Jewish parentage, demand that they be identified as Jewish. For those of mixed parentage, Jewishness may be an option, but for others it is a fact of life.

One common error in Jewish thinking is that people inherit their religion. A distinction must be made because, in fact, no child is born with a set of beliefs. Nevertheless, all children are born into families bound by their own ancestral and/or community cultures. Children inherit a culture that may or may not inculcate the religion of that culture.

WHAT ABOUT THE TERM "CONVERTED JEW"?

Most Jewish believers in Jesus feel uncomfortable with the term "converted Jew." The Hebrew verb for convert is *shuv*. It means to repent. We Jewish believers in Jesus are converts in that we have repented of our sin, but being Jewish was never a sin and we never repented of it. Our sin was that we didn't follow the Law God gave our people. We were unable to do that, and neither is anyone else able to do so. The only one who ever followed that Law perfectly was Jesus Christ. Somehow, mystically, when we are in Him and He is in us, we have fulfilled the Law. We are not converted Jews but converted sinners, and in Christ, we are completed Jews.

To find an answer to "Who is a Jew?" we must first state the question properly. Are Jews those who follow a particular religion? Are they citizens of a certain nation called Israel? Or are they identified as Jews by their racial-ethnic identification?

In a sense, all three descriptions apply, yet not exactly. Jews are a race, but not anthropologically separate. Jews come in all colors. In a sense, all Jews are people of Israel, but most of them were not born in that country, nor do most of them reside there. All Jews are Israelites but not all Israelites are Israelis. There is a Jewish religion, but many Jews don't follow that traditional religion.

Ask four Jewish people who or what is a Jew, and you may get five different answers. Yet consider this definition based on Scripture:

The Jews are those who, regardless of birth or religious beliefs, belong to the people with whom God established covenants through Abraham, Moses and David.

The Jewish community has always argued that if

those of us who are Jewish become Christians, we are no longer Jewish. We contend that as such people, we have become just the kind of Jews God wants us—and them—to be. We are Jewish by virtue of the fact that we belong to the people with whom God made the covenants through Abraham, Moses and David. No rabbi, no Jewish court, no consensus of people, can take away this God-given Jewishness. As for the Jewish religion, we can face our fellow Jews with a smile and say, "Jesus, the Jewish Messiah, made us kosher."

To the above scriptural definition of a Jew, we can add a practical description based on history:

A Jew may also be one who, though not born to Jewish parents, has, through a binding ritual of consent, joined the people with whom God established covenants through Abraham, Moses and David.

Both of these definitions depend on the word "covenant."

THE ABRAHAMIC COVENANT

God brought Abram out of Ur of the Chaldees. He changed Abram's name to Abraham and promised to make him the father of a great nation (Genesis 12:2). Abraham's progeny would be as numerous as the stars of heaven (15:5). God would give them the land of Canaan as their inheritance (15:18), and through them He would bring ultimate blessing to all nations (Genesis 12:3). From Abraham's son, Isaac, and grandson, Jacob, came the twelve tribes of Israel. They left Canaan during a great famine and settled in Egypt, where they stayed for 480 years.

THE MOSAIC COVENANT

The Israelites became enslaved while they were in Egypt, and God called Moses to lead them out of servitude. At Mount Sinai, God gave them the Law and promised again to give them the Land. Scripture tells us that God chose Israel from among all people, not because of any merit but because He loved her (Deuteronomy 7:7,8). She then belonged to God, and His earthly blessings were contingent on her obedience to His commandments.

THE DAVIDIC COVENANT

After forty years in the wilderness because of disobedience, Israel finally entered Canaan, the Promised Land. Moses died. Joshua, and after him various judges, ruled the people. Through the prophet Samuel, God acceded to Israel's desire for a king and appointed Saul. After Saul came David. Psalm 89:3,4 and 2 Samuel 7:12-16 record certain promises God made to King David. God promised His people a king in perpetuity. This king would be the Messiah, David's descendant, and would rule not only Israel but eventually all the nations. That promise reinforced God's covenant with Abraham that in his seed (the Jewish people) all the families of the earth would be blessed.

IF JEWS ALREADY HAVE A COVENANT WITH GOD, WHY DO THEY NEED JESUS?

God's covenants through Abraham, Moses and David contained promises of a peoplehood, a land and a King, the coming Savior. Those covenants never implied a personal salvation relationship with God. They neither depended on nor produced the salvation of those with whom God had made His covenant. Rather, God's earthly promises to the Jewish people were contingent on their service and obedience to Him. Professor David Larsen explains it succinctly:

From the Bible, the fact of when and how God

chose Israel seems clear. It all began with Abraham and the choice was God's alone. But why did He do it? Why did He make Israel His "firstborn son" (Exodus 4:22)? Moses put it rather simply to Israel: "It was because the Lord loved you" (Deuteronomy 7:8). But did that love have a purpose? The purpose of God's election was not salvation (as if the Lord gave some preferential claim to the Jews), but His purpose was service.

As H. H. Rowley emphasized, the divine potter is not an aimless dilettante. "The uniqueness of His choice of Israel was the uniqueness of the degree in which He purposed to reveal His character and His will through her, and for this she was supremely suited" (cf Exodus 19:3-6; Deuteronomy 5:2ff). The discipline of service is the corollary of election as the history of Israel discloses most impressively.[1]

On the other hand, the Bible specifically states that salvation depends not on obedience or service, but on God's grace to all who place their faith in Christ's vicarious atonement. "For by grace you have been saved through faith, and that not of yourselves; it is the gift of God, not of works, lest anyone should boast" (Ephesians 2:8). Acts 4:12 states: ". . . there is no other name under heaven given among men by which we must be saved" [Jesus Christ of Nazareth, cf 4:10]. Also Jesus Himself said, "I am the Way, the Truth and the Life; no man comes to the Father except by Me" (John 14:6).

The necessity is so obvious that it shouldn't need to be stated here. Yet in recent years some well-meaning Christians have been suggesting otherwise. They claim

---

[1]David L. Larsen, *Jews, Gentiles and the Church: A New Perspective on History and Prophecy* (Grand Rapids: Discovery House, 1995), 19. (Quoting from H.H. Rowley, The Biblical Doctrine of Election [London: Lutterwort, 1950]).

that all Jewish people have a separate covenant with God that excludes them from the New Covenant that Jesus brought.

There is no biblical basis for such an assumption! Jesus is the fulfillment of God's promise to David in 2 Samuel 7, and He is also the fulfillment of God's promise in Jeremiah 31:31 to make a new covenant with the House of Israel and the House of Judah. In every point of Jesus' teaching He referred to the Old Covenant—the Law and the words of the prophets. Yet He also said, "I bring to you a new commandment." When He said that, He was talking directly to the Jewish people of His day. They needed His work of atonement in order to be saved. Jewish people today still need Jesus as much as anyone else in order to be saved, and that should motivate you to witness to them.

A study of this book can help you understand Jewish people and provide you with valuable information that can help you in your witnessing. First, and very basic, is a description of the major branches of Judaism in Chapter 3.

CHAPTER 3

BASIC JUDAISM

There are three major branches of Judaism: Orthodox, Conservative and Reform. Christians, and many Jews, view the Conservative and Reform movements as merely lesser forms of the same religion. Each of these branches adheres to certain tenets and maintains its own emphasis, but the major differences pertain to liturgical practices rather than theology.

ORTHODOX JUDAISM

As much as possible, Orthodox Judaism preserves the ancient observances and traditions of the Fathers. Orthodox rabbis are usually trained in academies called yeshivas. An Orthodox rabbi would teach that strict adherence to the traditional liturgy enables a Jewish person to live a life based upon good ethics. Truly Orthodox Jews make a valiant attempt to keep the Law of Moses, but they would readily admit that the task is almost impossible. Confronted with this inevitable failure, they would maintain that a sincere desire to perform the religious duties counts more than the actual deeds. In one sense, the Orthodox rabbinic clergy follow the tradition of the Pharisees. Some of the Orthodox rabbis would hold a pro-life, anti-abortion position in line with evangelical Christian thought. Nevertheless, Orthodox Jews don't accept the Bible in the same way that evangelical Christians do. Orthodox Jews generally view the Bible as a holy book, but few would feel free to come to a personal interpretation of Scripture that differed from that of the rabbis. In this aspect, Orthodox Judaism comes closer to the Roman Catholic or Greek Orthodox traditions, which maintain that authoritative interpretation of Scripture must come through the Church.

REFORM JUDAISM

Reform Judaism doesn't use most of the liturgy that is so traditional among European Jewry. They conduct fewer of the worship services in Hebrew, have discarded much of the traditional forms and have deleted the Orthodox emphasis on the supernatural. The Reform Movement maximizes ethics and self-realization and places a minimal emphasis on the old liturgy of Judaism. Reform Jews consider the traditional laws and customs of their ancestors unimportant and often treat them as mere superstition. They seek to adapt their religious practices and objectives to the changing times. One poll showed that less than ten percent of all Reform rabbis believed in a "personal God" in any traditional sense. In doctrine, Reform Judaism bears a close resemblance to the Unitarian religion, which seems better known for what its adherents don't believe rather than for the faith they confess. Prominent among Reform Jewish seminaries in the United Sates are Hebrew Union College in Cincinnati, Ohio, and the University of Judaism of Los Angeles, California.

CONSERVATIVE JUDAISM

Conservative Judaism seeks to achieve a balance between ethics and liturgy. This branch of Judaism considers it wrong to overemphasize either the liturgical or the ethical aspects of the faith. Conservative Jews retain those elements they feel are meaningful and eliminate religious practices they consider too antiquated for this day and age. They seek to update religious practices and beliefs by using English translations and a few modern innovations that more Orthodox Jews would consider inappropriate. As with the Reform movement, the Conservative movement tends to de-emphasize the supernatural. Conservative Judaism has approximately two million adherents in the United States and is the fastest growing of the three major movements. Most Conservative synagogues and temples are found in suburban areas, where many Jews are moving. Conservative Judaism trains its religious leaders at Conservative Theological Seminary of America in New York City.

In addition to the three major branches of Judaism, we see a few minor offshoots.

MINOR OFFSHOOTS:
Humanistic Judaism

Humanistic Judaism is a self-proclaimed secular movement founded in 1969 in Farmington, Michigan by Sherwin T. Wine. The movement proclaims itself to be part of the "Secular Revolution" and "a clear alternative to rabbinic Judaism." It is a Judaism without God, affirming the importance of Jewish identity and presenting itself as an alternative to traditional theistic Judaism.

The Reconstructionist Movement

The Reconstructionist movement is a branch of the Conservative movement. Reconstructionist rabbis are trained at Reconstruction Rabbinical Seminary in Philadelphia, Pennsylvania. Reconstructionism maintains that since Judaism is a culture and a way of life as well as a religion, it is a religious civilization. As such, it requires constant adaptation to contemporary conditions, so that Jews can identify more readily and significantly with the Jewish community.

The Chassidic Movement

The Chassidic Movement is ultra-orthodox. Its adherents are strict in every aspect of their religion, especially in keeping the Law of Moses. Because of its mystical qualities and missionary zeal, this group is growing, especially among young Jews. The Chassidic movement is essentially separatist and avoids social relationships with non-Jews. Chassidic Jews venerate their rabbis and view them as miracle workers. The "Rebbes," as these leaders are called, regulate all facets of life within the Chassidic community.

Zionism

Zionism is sometimes mistakenly considered a religious movement. It is essentially a political movement concerned with a return to the land of Israel rather than with any religious ideology. Yet the Zionists have always been motivated with a zeal that made them seem very religious.

Messianic Judaism

Perhaps we should also mention here the messianic Jews who worship Jesus as Messiah and are truly Christians. Because of their desire to maintain a strong Jewish identity and not become Gentilized as much of the Church has, messianic Jews use terminology that differs from that used in most Gentile churches, and they weave Hebraic concepts into their worship. More will be said about this later.

SUMMING UP. . .

Here's an easy way to remember the Jewish denominations:

- Liken Orthodox Judaism to Roman Catholicism or the Greek Orthodox Church, both of which place great emphasis on tradition.
- Liken Reform Judaism to Unitarianism, with an emphasis on humanism.
- Liken Conservative Judaism to modern liberal Protestantism, which emphasizes form more than doctrinal content.

There is no equivalent in Judaism to fundamentalist or evangelical Christian churches that emphasize a personal relationship with God in accordance with the Bible. Orthodox Judaism is sometimes mistakenly seen that way, but it is more concerned with living in a traditional way according to the precepts and interpretations of the rabbis, who are doctrinally related to the ancient Pharisees and really hold no concept of a personal relationship with God.

A DIFFERENCE IN WITNESSING?

In witnessing to Jewish people, does it matter to which branch of Judaism they belong? It can be a small factor, but generally it will not be as important as a denominationally-oriented Gentile might believe. That's because it's not necessarily true that a person who identifies with a particular synagogue holds strictly to the tenets of that denomination. For the most part, Jews today join a synagogue for reasons other than doctrine. These include proximity to their homes, having friends or relatives who attend, or the eloquence or social outlook of the presiding rabbi.

In an article published in a popular Jewish magazine, one rabbi stated that most of those who attend synagogue do not take the teachings seriously. He said that they have little interest in Talmudic ethics or philosophy of religion; rather, they are seeking the pragmatic value of some religious affiliation and the accompanying peace of mind they hope it will produce. He pointed out that ideological differences are of little concern to the average worshiper.

WITNESSING PRINCIPLES

All of this should help you establish certain principles in witnessing to Jewish people. Deal with individuals and not with their denomination or affiliation. Don't categorize Jews you know; chances are you will be wrong. Don't be surprised if the Jewish person you know has no denominational orientation; many Jews do not affiliate with a synagogue or temple, and most of those who do affiliate attend infrequently.

Most Jewish people confuse religious obligations with moral imperatives. Relatively few Jews believe that the Scriptures are the Word of God and that they have an obligation to study them in order to determine what God requires of them as individuals. Many Jews give nominal assent to the Bible but do not believe that they have an obligation to obey its teachings. They don't question the truthfulness of Scripture, but if they keep the Sabbath or abstain from pork or shellfish, they do so because their heritage as Jews demands it, not because they feel that God commands it.

Some Jews hold an anti-supernatural view of the Bible. They consider the recorded miracles and revelations as mere fables, yet they feel they must maintain the moral and ethical teachings of the Old Testament. They go through the Bible like shoppers in a supermarket, selecting from the shelves only what they want and bypassing the rest.

Many Jews claim to be atheists or agnostics and are anti-religious. Because of their cultural heritage they, like most of their Jewish counterparts, become deeply involved in contemporary causes. Because they have accepted the moral-social values of the Bible, they are concerned with the need for social justice. For the most part, they would admit that they are somewhat confused about religion because even the rabbis often contradict one another's views. Such Jews may or may not believe that there is a God, but they doubt that they or anyone else has the ability to know. Consequently, concepts of God and His will are moot questions to them.

Despite such differences, a certain mystique exists that binds all Jews together in such a way that they cannot forsake their Jewishness.

The important factor in your witness to Jewish people will be what views they hold. Do they believe the Bible is a book of myths? Do they consider it partially true? Do they consider it the revealed Word of God? What role do they assign to God, the Bible and religion in their own lives?

Your Christian witness can only begin when people come to the realization that there is a God and that He requires something from them. You must demonstrate this fact and your listener must accept it before a witness can proceed.

UNDERSTANDING SENSITIVITIES

Your Jewish contacts will seem to you much the same as their Gentile social counterparts. Outwardly they are, because historically the need for survival has required us Jews to learn to fit in. Nevertheless, we are different. There are differences in culture that are not so readily apparent. There are also differences in social attitudes that may be the result of our past struggles to stay alive while compressed into ghettos and suffering economic disadvantage.

Don't make the mistake of thinking that Jews are "just like anyone else." Jews don't see themselves that way. They don't respond to the gospel "just like anyone else."

A JEWISH VIEW OF CHRISTIANITY

To Jews, Christianity is "the religion of the Gentiles," and because of past persecution, Gentile motives toward Jews are under suspicion.

Herman Wouk, a well-known Jewish author, portrays the feeling that most Jews have about Gentiles: that underneath it all, most non-Jews harbor a tinge of resentment against Jewish people. In his book *This Is My God*, Wouk puts it this way:

> Get two non-Jews confiding in each other, after cautiously finding that they have enough

27

common ground not to mistake each other for the kind of mental defective called an anti-Semite, and they are likely to agree that notwithstanding all this liberal talk, Jews tend to be brash, pushing, sharp in business, vulgar in manners, loud in public, and so clannish that they band in a knot against the Christian world. They will also agree that they know Jews who are different, and that they number such Jews among their valued friends. There are, of course, many Christians who will take no part in such an exchange. But the reader will recognize the common places.[2]

Wouk might be surprised to find out that non-Jews in Iowa, New Hampshire and South Carolina spend very little time thinking about the Jewish people. Many have never met a Jew; most are not even very curious. However, because Jews spend a great deal of time thinking about their Jewishness, they presume that it is also a topic of conversation among non-Jews. Books like *This Is My God* and many of the modern novels about Jewish people are invaluable to the Christian who wants to know about the Jews and Jewish thinking. It will be a help to you and your witnessing not only to read such books but also to be alert to newspaper and magazine articles about the Jews.

The Jewish people are unique in history, culture and outlook. Because of these differences, Jewish evangelism must be different. It must speak to a people who live within a certain cultural framework. Jewish culture is different from all other non-Christian cultures inasmuch as it is based on a religious

---

[2]Herman Wouk, *This Is My God* (New York, NY: Doubleday, 1959), 28.

framework of God-given holiday celebrations, dietary laws and the Bible. The entire Law was designed to keep the Jewish people separated from their Gentile neighbors and unto God. Now, even though Jewish people may not keep the Law, most of them feel a need to be separate.

JEWISHNESS IS A WAY OF LIFE

Jewishness is more than a religion. It is a way of life, a way of relating one to another. It's good to read the writings of the rabbis, but when you compare them with the writings of contemporary Jewish novelists, you will realize that a wide gap exists between the ideals of the rabbis and real Jewish life today. The common Jewish viewpoint on religion is far removed from that of the Jewish clergyman, although there do remain some points of agreement.

While Christianity is a redemptive religion, concerned first with the problem of sin and salvation, and subsequently with how to live the Christian life, present-day Judaism is a moral religion. As such, it is concerned with how to live and maintain a Jewish identity. Jewish religious thinkers and Jewish people on the street tend to presume redemption or salvation. They don't think about gaining eternal life or avoiding hell. If they think about sin at all, they think about it in terms of evil deeds by which they have wronged others. Even if Jews fail to observe the Sabbath or break the dietary laws, they are apt to be more concerned about letting their grandparents down than about offending God.

The average Jew is not likely to attend religious services as frequently as the non-Jew. Jews regard their temples or synagogues as the fountainheads of their religion, but they may not personally feel a need for religion. What Jewish people are primarily seeking from their religion, if anything, is a discovery of their own identity and help in working out some of the mysterious inner feelings they can only account for by the fact that they are Jewish.

JEWS PRESUME A STANDING WITH GOD

Jews presume a standing with God by virtue of their ancestry. They see their chief duty to Him as that of living a life worthy of their Jewish heritage. Because of this, they feel it is of the utmost importance to preserve their identity as Jews and to take a stand on behalf of Jewish survival. In the synagogue they might gain the rationale for separation from other people. The synagogue might provide answers to certain metaphysical problems. It might be able to answer the question "What is a Jew?" and supply motivation to do the Jewish thing. However a Jew might choose to do the Jewish thing through organizations other than religious institutions. The synagogue might help to define imperatives and develop a sense of Jewish consciousness, but after all, the Jewish community offers an individual so many options, such as charities, social causes, etc. A Jewish person can only choose a few of these and might well decide to follow some of them outside of the synagogue.

THE WE-THEY SYNDROME

Most Jewish people envision a we-they relationship with regard to the Christian community. That is because Jews automatically assume that all Gentiles are Christians. They don't realize that a distinction exists between truly committed followers of Jesus and the Gentile persecutors of the Jews down through the ages. To Jews, Hitler, the leaders of the Spanish Inquisition and evangelists like

Billy Graham fall into the same category. They are not Jewish, so they must be Christians. Therefore, for a Jew to believe in Jesus Christ, "their" God, is to go over to the side of the "enemy."

The basic point Christians must understand is that even though Jewish people may not be able to define what it means to be a Jew, they feel an obligation of loyalty to their people always to remain Jewish. A Jew's honor and personhood depend on that loyalty. Jews have been taught from the cradle that Judaism and Christianity are mutually exclusive categories—that when Jews accept Christ, they have deserted their people and are no longer Jewish. Therefore, Jewish people feel they must resist the claims of Christ.

CHAPTER 5

BE ENCOURAGED TO WITNESS— JEWS ARE COMING TO CHRIST!

You already know that the gospel of salvation is for all people, and that certainly includes the Jews. You care about Jewish people finding Christ, or you probably wouldn't be reading this book. The following vignettes describe several Jewish people from various backgrounds and levels of religious commitment who gave their lives to Jesus. We hope these accounts will motivate and encourage you even more to share the good news of Jesus with Jewish people.

ANDREW

Andrew, a young Jewish man from New York, was into science and logic and had discarded his early religious training as needless superstition. Then Andrew's friend and part-time employer at college told him that Jesus was his Savior. She also gave him a Bible—which he set aside for an entire year. Andrew couldn't understand why his friend thought Jesus was for Jews, but her life impressed him. She lived differently from everyone he knew and always acted like God was watching her.

A book called *God and the Astronomers* further piqued Andrew's interest in spiritual matters. Then Andrew's friend gave him a Jews for Jesus pamphlet. Andrew contacted Jews for Jesus Headquarters. A staff member put him in touch with a missionary who would be preaching in Andrew's hometown. Before leaving the area, the missionary introduced Andrew to another Jewish believer who further influenced him through Bible studies and prayer.

As a space science major, Andrew was spending much time in the observatory. There he began thinking about the vastness of the universe and the God who had created it all. At first, he couldn't believe that the One who coordinated the cosmos could care personally for His creatures. Yet one day, remembering Scriptures he had been shown, Andrew admitted that God wanted to be involved in his life and had sent Jesus to save him. Andrew gave his heart to Jesus and subsequently gave up his profession in astronomy to become a Jews for Jesus missionary.

NORMAN

Norman, a Jewish policeman from Detroit, couldn't forget a terrible nightmare he had experienced. He had felt immersed in darkness and knew he had died. An eyeless, satanic figure with a horrible grin had confronted him, but then another figure seemed to hover over him and fight for him with a double-edged sword.

About the same time, Norman's partner became a Christian, and Norman began to notice changes in him—the partner began to carry a Bible and cleaned up his life. Months later, he asked Norman to help with volunteer security at a Billy Graham crusade. When Norman met Billy Graham and shook his hand, he felt instantaneous relief from the excruciating pain of a recent arm injury. Amazed, he could only think, "Oh, God! This kind of healing only happens to Gentiles. What's going on? I need to talk to someone." A police sergeant who was also a minister was standing nearby. When Norman described what had happened, he said, "Don't let Satan rob you of what the Lord did for you today. God is revealing Himself to you." Norman took his advice and began looking into what the Bible said. In a second dream (or vision), Norman saw a white-robed, smiling figure and was deeply moved. He discussed the spiritual import of his two visions with this minister, who helped him interpret them in light of certain Scripture passages. Within weeks, Norman prayed to give his life to the Lord.

VERA

Vera, a young Holocaust survivor, came to the United States where she obtained citizenship and began to study medicine. Vera felt that God had spared her from the Nazis to fulfill her destiny, but she didn't know much about Him. She retained her simple belief in God and eventually felt she must investigate her faith more fully. During her residency, Vera discussed religion with her roommate, a practicing Catholic who asked her questions about Judaism. Vera had trouble explaining how she knew her sins were forgiven and admitted that uncertainty in her life. Searching for answers, she took a trip to Israel, attended temple and began reading the Bible, both Old and New Testaments. One day she read Isaiah 53 and thought it sounded like Jesus. She decided it had been changed in the "Christian" Bible. Yet when she read the same passage from the Bible at temple, though some of the words were different, the message was the same.

Through her pediatric practice, Vera met a Christian couple who came to her with their infant son. Vera was impressed with their sweet spirit and obvious lives of faith. The husband was a Baptist minister. Slowly Vera and this couple became friends. She spent a great deal of time with them and even visited their vacation home on weekends. She let them know that she was reading the Bible because she wanted them to understand that she, too, was religious in her own way. Then one day she asked them, "How can anyone know what is the right religion?" The minister responded, "I knew when I accepted the Messiah as my personal Savior." That made Vera aware of two points: first, that Christians believed in Jesus as the Jewish Messiah, and second, that a person is not born a "Christian." Then her friend asked her a question: "What happened to the sacrifices for sin in the Jewish religion?" Vera didn't know but determined she would find out.

Vera asked a Jewish friend, but her friend's answer was unsatisfactory. She continued to pray, to read the Bible and to wonder. Then one day, Vera's Christian friends invited her to attend church. The pastor's sermon was on the first Psalm, but toward the end he talked about John 14:6 where Jesus said, "I am the Way, the Truth and the Life. No man comes to the Father except through Me." Vera was offended at that, but the words seemed to haunt her. She began to read her old Jewish prayer book as well as the Bible. Certain passages impressed her, but she was not ready to take the leap of faith. Then one weekend, while visiting her Christian friends again, Vera went to bed with many questions and a prayer in her heart that

God would show her the truth. She awoke early the next morning and knew that God was telling her that Jesus was the Messiah and that she must believe and obey. With Vera's prayer of commitment to Y'shua, her long search was over.

HENRY

Henry, a Jewish airline pilot, was troubled by the deaths of young soldiers in Viet Nam and the suicide of an actress he had met in Palm Springs. Unable to cope with the reality of death, he deliberately got himself fired by the airline company so he could go off to Hawaii to "turn on, tune in and drop out." Henry wanted to free himself of material entrapments and "get back to the earth." As he pondered how he might find God, he decided to go back to his Jewish roots. To him, that meant a trip to Israel. He imagined he would find a spiritually aware group of people there. Instead, he was greatly disappointed to find a largely secular majority who was forced by a religious minority to observe the Jewish Law. Henry visited Israel several more times without finding the answers he sought. Subsequent adventures took Henry to Alaska, then the South Seas and finally back to Hawaii, where he investigated eastern religions. Periodically he became interested in some new guru but found no lasting satisfaction in any of their teachings. He still hungered for spiritual truth and kept on searching.

Henry proposed to Janet, a girl from his past with whom he had previously had a serious relationship. They were married, but within six weeks, Henry realized that he couldn't handle such a commitment. Six months later, the marriage ended in divorce. Taking stock of his life, Henry realized that he was not the nice guy he had thought himself to be. He felt confusion, loneliness and futility. From time to time he would cry out, "God, if you're real, please reveal yourself to me."

One day while jogging, Henry met a woman named Mary. They became friends, and during a car trip together, Henry began a conversation with Mary about what she considered important in life. Mary said she was a "born-again" Christian. She was very excited about Jesus and tried to tell Henry about Him, but Henry didn't want to hear it. Mary stopped talking. Later she began to read her Bible aloud. Henry stopped her, saying that he wasn't interested. Again, Mary complied with his wishes, but she began silently praying that God would bring someone into Henry's life who would tell him about Jesus.

A half hour later, they stopped at a junk yard to search for a used car part. The junk yard owner said something to Henry about Jesus returning and began to quote to him from the Bible. Henry was angry, but Mary was amazed at such a quick answer to her prayer. Despite Henry's determination not to listen, the man's demeanor and the words he spoke struck a responsive chord. The message went straight to Henry's heart and reached the empty spot he had been aching to fill. Returning to the car, he told Mary, "Half an hour ago, I told you that if your Bible could speak to my heart, I might believe. I know that man was sent to tell me those words." Mary read to Henry again from the Bible, and this time he knew that he was hearing God's words. Further down the road, Henry picked up a hitchhiker, and that man was also a Christian. He, too, pulled out a little Bible, and for the fourth time that day, Henry heard the Word of God read to him. Before the hitchhiker left, he told Henry, "I feel in my heart that you are ready to accept Jesus as your Lord and Savior."

Henry wasn't quite sure what that meant, but something inside told him that he was indeed ready. He went home and went to sleep. The next morning, listening to his car radio, Henry heard a gospel song that touched his heart. Suddenly he felt the weight of his sins and realized his need for the redemption only Jesus could bring. Driving along in the car, he prayed, "Jesus, please come into my life and take away my sin."

JACK

Jack, a successful Jewish oncologist, wondered if his medical practice, his comfortable family life and their acceptance in the community were all the good he could expect out of life. Was there anything more? Jack and his wife, Marilyn, tried everything from disco dancing to getting involved in a local Jewish temple, but all seemed empty and meaningless. Then Jack developed a serious eye condition and lashed out at God, "Who are You? What are You like? Why are You doing this to me when so many people that You gave cancer to depend on me? You must not exist!" Jack's health stabilized. During that time, he encountered many cancer patients who seemed to have answers for their dire circumstances. They didn't seem to feel the anger toward God that Jack had experienced. He knew that they believed in Jesus and trusted Him. When some of them tried to tell Jack about their faith, he wouldn't listen. How could they trust Him when He had allowed such pain and suffering in their lives? Jack envied their faith but figured it didn't matter. After all, Jesus wasn't for Jews, only for Gentiles. At the same time, Marilyn was going through a similar process, but Jack didn't know this because they never discussed their inner spiritual struggles.

One day, Jack learned that another Jewish physician

and his family were attending a Christian church. Outraged, Jack called to confront him. The physician said that he had found his Judaism and the God of Judaism at this church and was now, for the first time, truly proud and excited to be Jewish. Jack was shocked but curious and went to that church to see for himself what it was all about. The sermon dealt with Psalm 73, in which Asaph, a pious Jew, asks why good people suffer and evil people prosper. Jack couldn't believe the topic. How could they have known at the church that he had those same questions? He sat there and received the answer that God sees all from an eternal perspective, while we see everything from an immediate, present viewpoint. Those who believe and belong to God are His for eternity, but those who are not God's will spend forever having had nothing except the temporary pleasures of this short life. Jack walked into that church as an agnostic/atheist/skeptic and walked out knowing that God was real, good and worthy to be loved and worshiped. All he had to do was find out who He really was. He determined to follow this God, whoever He was, but he hoped it wasn't Jesus!

Jack and Marilyn spent the next three hours talking to the Jewish physician and his wife who had invited them to church. These friends explained how Judaism and Christianity fit together, how Jesus fulfilled the messianic prophecies of the Old Testament and that Christians were really worshiping the Messiah of Judaism. They talked about sin and separation from God and Jesus being God's cure.

It all made so much sense to Jack, but he felt he must ask a rabbi about it. He tried several rabbis, but none could explain away Christian theology as it would apply to a Jew. Jack found their reasoning flawed and shallow. The more he studied, the more he wanted to have this oneness with God that his friends had—but he was told it could only come from a relationship with Jesus, a commitment he was still fighting. A couple of months later, however, both Jack and Marilyn made separate decisions to repent of sin and commit their lives to Jesus as Lord and Savior. They found that Jesus filled the void that nothing else could ever fill.

CEIL

Ceil, a 19-year-old Jewish atheist, decided to return to her childhood faith in God. Raised in an Orthodox home, she had learned Hebrew and all the Jewish traditions and prayers. She had been taught that the Jews were special to God, that one day He would send a Messiah to rescue them from their earthly troubles, and that she must obey the Torah, the Law of Moses. Her early life had been governed by the strictness of Orthodox Judaism. As a child, she had complied, but during her teens she had rebelled against a religion that seemed to foster no intimacy with a God who demanded such strict obedience. Along with the toys of her childhood, Ceil had discarded the dietary laws and the Sabbath regulations. Finally she had taken her rebellion a step further and had claimed to be an atheist.

Now married, in her own home, with a child on the way and the freedom to choose what she would believe, Ceil admitted to herself that God existed. She felt no need then to return to Orthodox Judaism because she hadn't decided who God was or what, if anything, He required of her. She simply prayed, "God, I'm sorry I said you didn't exist. I know that you do. Thank you for my husband, my home and the baby we're expecting—and please let this child be healthy." She thought no more about religion until her little daughter was about two months old.

At home a great deal with the new baby, Ceil spent much time listening to music. To welcome her home from the hospital, Ceil's husband had bought her a record player and several music albums. One album was Christmas music, which Ceil had always surreptitiously enjoyed, though she always avoided singing the name of Jesus.

Ceil began to listen to the carols and was struck by words she seemed to be hearing for the first time: "O, little town of Bethlehem, how still we see thee lie. Above thy deep and dreamless sleep, the silent stars go by. Yet in thy dark streets shineth the Everlasting Light. The hopes and fears of all the years are met in thee tonight." She wondered, "What were those hopes and fears? Did they have anything to do with the Jewish hope for a Messiah? Did they allude to the fact that maybe Jewish people were afraid to think that Jesus might have been the Messiah?" Only once before, during a Christmas pageant in high school, had Ceil ever thought about the words of a Christmas carol. Her choral group had sung, "Oh come, oh come Emmanuel, and ransom captive Israel, that mourns in lonely exile here until the Son of God appear." At the time she had briefly wondered whether or not Jesus was the Messiah whom God was supposed to send, but she had quickly dismissed the thought. After all, she had decided that God didn't exist, so how could any of this matter?

Now, years later, having admitted that God did exist, Ceil found the memory of that first song, together with the words of "Little Town of Bethlehem" and "We Three Kings" compelling her to think about Jesus. She prayed, "God, please show me if there is any truth in what Christians say about Jesus. I'm ready to do what you want me to do. Do you want me to go back to Orthodox Judaism and keep all the laws and traditions, or do you want me to believe in Jesus?" As she prayed, the baby woke up and needed attention. Ceil forgot about her prayer until several days later when in the night sky she saw a large, brilliant star. It reminded her of the Christmas star and made her wonder, "Am I beginning to believe that it really happened? Should I read the New Testament and find out for myself about Jesus?" Though previously afraid to read the "Gentile" Bible, she succumbed after many months to her growing curiosity. Provoked by a constant nudging from God, she began to read the New Testament.

Those Holy Spirit nudges were God's answer to the prayers of Orville, a Gentile Christian friend of Ceil's husband. Orville had met Ceil's husband at a streetcar stop, had witnessed to him and had gotten a seemingly negative response. He stopped witnessing to Ceil's husband, but kept on praying—for three years. About the time Ceil decided that she believed in Jesus and needed someone with whom she could talk, God moved Orville to ask a local missionary to visit her. The missionary taught Ceil and was instrumental in getting her to a church where she made a commitment to Jesus.

Ceil began praying and witnessing to her husband, and a few months later, he also came to faith. If you don't already know, that young Jewish wife's husband was Moishe Rosen, founder of Jews for Jesus, an organization that has been instrumental in bringing many—both Jews and Gentiles—to Christ.

Of course, the glory belongs to God, not to Moishe or to Jews for Jesus. Yet what if that one brave young Christian had not witnessed to one Jew and, despite apparent rejection, prayed for him for three years?

What if Orville had given up when Moishe responded, "It's okay for you to believe, but as for me, I'm a Jew!"? What if Orville and his family had not persisted in prayer for Moishe for three years? Certainly God could have used someone else to witness to Moishe or to some other future leader in Jewish evangelism. In any case, Orville would have missed the blessing of becoming a link in something important that God wanted to accomplish.

A COMMON THREAD

Though the details vary, a common thread runs through these stories. All of them, even those that contain supernatural experiences, show how God used people who already knew Him to help bring unbelievers to saving faith in Jesus. A few were professional ministers, but many were ordinary lay Christians—like you. Here's the bottom line: if you are willing to be God's instrument, He can use you!

Interested? Want to know how? Read on. The following chapters will help you learn how to witness to Jewish people and everyone else who needs to know Jesus, the Jewish Messiah.

CHAPTER 6

THE FENCE OF OFFENSE

Our understanding of the gospel is influenced strongly by the cultural "lens" through which we have been seeing it all our lives. What we see clearly through our particular lens will not appear as clearly—if it appears at all—to those who do not share our orientation. In attempting to communicate gospel truth to people equipped with a cultural "lens" other than ours, we should, as much as possible, employ a manner and language that create the best possible understanding.

Don't be afraid to witness to people who belong to cultures that generally resist Christianity. It's your duty. They don't have to like you. You're not trying to win them to yourself; you are trying to win them to the Lord. Nevertheless, effective cross-cultural communication to a dissimilar ethnic or gospel-resistant group requires a great deal of discernment.

Unfortunately, there are several areas where Christians may unconsciously and unintentionally offend Jewish people. This may be due to differences in culture or to a lack of sensitivity to Jewish thinking on certain matters. Whatever the cause, the effect is to raise a barrier instead of build a relationship where communication can begin.

CULTURAL DIFFERENCES

To the Jewish eye, evangelical Christians may appear somewhat dour and puritanical. Some Jewish people are repelled by the all too apparent austerity of some Christians because, to a degree, it violates Jewish sensitivities.

A good example of a cultural difference is manner of dress. Christian good taste calls for modesty and neatness; generally, Jewish people would agree on the importance of neatness, but they would choose attractiveness over what they might regard as a prudish appearance. Many Christians who are oriented to a mid-country rural lifestyle might regard urbane East or West Coast Jews as too ostentatious, while the same Jews might consider those Christians too plain.

Another area where cultural differences exist is that of weddings. Picture the most spartan kind of Christian wedding reception: Well-groomed but conservatively dressed wedding guests mill about or gather in small groups in the fellowship hall of a church, nibbling the traditional wedding cake, salted nuts and pastel-colored mints. They sip coffee or punch as they greet friends. Occasionally the low murmur of conversation is punctuated by polite laughter or the squeals of a few excited teenagers. The most boisterous occurrence is usually the departure of the newlyweds amidst showers of rice or confetti, and the reception is over in an hour or two.

Contrast this scene with a typical Jewish wedding reception (an event for which the bride's family may have been saving from her infancy!): Elaborately dressed friends and relatives raise their voices in cheerful greetings above the din of an orchestra that is alternately playing hora tunes and contemporary music; waiters in formal attire nimbly skirt the dance floor as they serve a sit-down meal or endlessly refill hot and cold buffet dishes. The festivities and music continue for hours, only to be interrupted from time to time by the master of ceremonies as he tells a joke, reads aloud a newly delivered telegram or proposes a toast.

Admittedly, the first scene is an extreme, but sometimes it does happen that way. The illustration was chosen to make a point: Those with limited means should never feel apologetic for providing just a simple wedding celebration, but most Jewish families would be deeply embarrassed not to host a lavish wedding. They would rather have just a private ceremony for the immediate family than invite many friends for whom they could not provide an extravagant affair. Can you begin to see the wideness of this culture gap?

While basic morals and ethics remain the same, a larger chasm exists that does not involve right and wrong. Rather, it involves what is considered good or bad taste. In Jewish circles, people tend to be more sophisticated and worldly in their outlook than the average evangelical Christian.

I think of a particular instance where a Christian who wanted to show his concern for some Jewish people attended a Jewish funeral. He was somewhat taken aback by a Jewish ritual that takes place after the funeral service at the home of the deceased. It involves a meal for the mourners that begins with the ceremonial breaking of bread and drinking of wine. That Christian had scruples against using alcohol as a beverage and did not realize that he was in the midst of a ceremony. He refused the wine that was handed to him with the declaration that as a Christian, he felt that all drinking of alcohol was wrong. He then cited several Bible verses. In that situation, it would have been far better if he had just touched the glass to his lips and put it back on the tray, rather than try to preach to the bereaved family about Christian separation.

In witnessing, watch your manners. Too many people "bear witness" as though they were religious authorities. That can be deadly. It is best to treat others with respect. Remember that you can't teach someone something unless he or she has agreed to be your student.

Jewish culture differs in other ways as well. Because of racial experience, Jewish humor tends more toward irony. Modern Jews don't make much of the Sabbath, but they do celebrate religious holidays in an elaborate manner. Jews have more ritual celebrations than Christians. Some of them—like circumcisions, confirmations (bar/bat mitzvahs) and, as already mentioned, weddings—are major occasions for which a Jewish family might even mortgage their home.

To Jews, Christian events often seem sterile, preachy and starkly ceremonial. Jews always feel like outsiders at such events. In the same way, most Christians feel like outsiders at Jewish celebrations.

Worship style is another area where cultural differences exist. In the United States, the evangelical Church has taken on certain extrabiblical values. In some churches, the preacher is not considered spiritual unless he proclaims his message in a loud voice with strong emotional tones, and the congregation is not thought to be reacting in a spiritual fashion unless it responds with loud, approving "amens" and "hallelujahs." Of course this is not true of all churches. Nevertheless, whether or not a congregation is accustomed to responding with hallelujahs and amens, they generally don't walk about, talk or whisper among themselves during the service unless absolutely necessary. In Jewish synagogues and temples, however, just the opposite happens. People move about freely during the liturgy but usually sit quietly and make no visible or audible response during the rabbi's sermon.

To show reverence during prayer, Christians have adopted the practice of bowed heads, closed eyes, clasped hands and perhaps a kneeling position. Jewish people identify those postures of prayer with all idolatrous systems. To show reverence, Jews do the opposite. They pray standing, with eyes open and heads covered.

A rabbi and a pastor speak quite differently from the pulpit. The rabbi will strive to maintain an assured tone of voice. He will cite only a small amount of Scripture in his sermon and will use only an occasional illustration but many opinions of the rabbis. On the other hand, an evangelical Christian sermon is usually replete with Scripture and illustrations. It contains few, if any, opinions from other churchmen and is delivered in a proclamatory tone. The rabbi wants to be eloquent and appear wise; the evangelical preacher wants to be relevant and urgent.

Synagogue services usually last longer than church services. Synagogue Scripture readings are part of the liturgy and are much longer than those in church services (as much as six chapters at a time). Also, in Orthodox and most Conservative synagogues, most of the congregation doesn't understand the Scripture readings because they are read in Hebrew.

The Christian communion service that is derived from the Jewish Passover feast contains very little that would remind a Jewish person of that holiday. Communion entails much solemn ceremony with a minute suggestion of food and drink. A modern Passover celebration, on the other hand, entails just the opposite. Generally, it includes a huge, elaborate meal with as little ritual as is possible in good conscience.

Another major cultural problem in presenting the gospel to Jewish people is the Christian portrayal of Jesus. Christian artists, teachers and preachers have frequently portrayed Jesus in their own ethnic, Gentile framework. The blue-eyed, fair-skinned Jesus painted by many artists is a stranger to the Jews. Though in recent years some artists have tried to correct this image, a problem still remains: Jewish people shun the use of visuals in worship. To a Jew, pictures, crosses and the like suggest "graven images," which were specifically forbidden in the Ten Commandments.

Politics is another example of cultural difference. Jewish people tend to be more liberal in their political persuasions than their Gentile socio-economic counterparts. This may be due to the emphasis on social justice by the Hebrew prophets or to centuries of being an oppressed minority. Jews also tend to seek causes and projects that will elevate people socially, educationally and economically.

JEWS DON'T UNDERSTAND CHRISTIAN DECLARATIONS OF LOVE

Christians can be too effusive in declaring their love for the Jewish people. Many evangelicals make the mistake of telling Jewish people, "We Christians love the Jews." Jews would find this a startling declaration, since they are very mindful of anti-Semitism. One well-meaning Christian woman told someone, "We Christians love the Jews because they gave us the Bible and the Savior." Her listener simply could not identify with that. He personally had never intended to give the Bible to anyone, and as far as the Savior was concerned, he didn't believe that Christ was the Savior. The woman's declaration of love found no response in that Jewish man's heart.

Don't try to affirm Jewish people by telling them that you love them. Instead, show them your love by your actions of kindness and consideration!

JEWS FIND CERTAIN WORDS OFFENSIVE

The way that you address people in your conversations is also important. Sometimes a Christian will make the mistake of speaking in the second person, plural: "You Jews are still looking for the coming of the Messiah." Not all Jews are looking for the coming of the Messiah, and the hearer resents the term "You Jews." Jewish people want to be dealt with as individuals rather than as a class or race of people. When it's necessary to mention the Jewish people as a group, it is always better to speak in the third person. Talk about "the Jewish people" rather than "you Jews."

Another area of offense is the Gentile tendency to refer to the female gender as a "Jewess." This is a patronizing and demeaning term, even though some Jewish people might use it to describe themselves. A better term is "Jewish girl" or "Jewish woman." In general, when speaking of the Jewish people, say "the Jewish people" rather than "the Jews," and when speaking about a male Jewish person, use the term "Jewish man" or "Jewish boy." Rather than talk about "a Jew I know," say "an acquaintance of mine who is Jewish."

The term Jewish as an adjective should never be used to describe anything other than the people, land, religion or language. If you talk about "Jewish money," "Jewish bankers," or "Jewish control of the media," you might well be guilty of anti-Semitic attitudes.

Whenever possible, avoid the words "missionary" or "mission." Jewish people associate such terms with the dregs of society who need a rescue mission, with primitive people who need medical or technological help, or worse yet, with people or groups who get paid to snatch unsuspecting souls away from their own faith.

Certain Christian jargon also produces a negative emotional valence in many Jewish people. The list includes words such as born again, blood of the Lamb, holy trinity, cross, church, convert, Christian, Savior and saved. To a Christian, these words are comforting symbols of faith. To believers the cross might be a symbol of God's love, but to most Jews, it is a symbol of an alien religion which has often persecuted Jews in the past. In witnessing to Jewish people, avoid using "hymnbook" language and metaphors, and stick with the kind of rhetoric that can be found in your daily newspaper.

Be sure that you don't behave patronizingly in your speech. Many non-Jews who try to talk to Jewish people think that they will communicate better by using a Hebrew word or even a few Yiddish words. Unfortunately, few people have enough of an ear for language to pronounce foreign words correctly; and even if they do pronounce foreign words correctly, it conveys the idea that they have a real knowledge of Hebrew or whatever language they're using. It's better to use language that you know and use well.

Here's another caution. You will surely be suspected of being anti-Semitic if you tell Jewish jokes to Jews. Jewish people do tell many jokes about themselves, but they don't know how to react to such jokes when they come from non-Jews. The "Rabbi, Priest and Protestant Minister" stories usually have the rabbi behaving in a stereotypical manner and talking with a heavy Yiddish accent. By telling those kinds of jokes to Jews, you may cause them to think that you are ridiculing them.

LEADERS SHOULD NOT BE CRITICIZED

Never, under any circumstances, criticize Jewish leaders. It's not that leaders in the Jewish community are above criticism, but if you want to be friends with Jewish people, don't make or accept from them that sort of statement about Jewish leaders. Your Jewish friends might be testing you to see if their expressions represent your sentiments. For example, if your Jewish friend says, "The rabbis are only interested in money and what they can get," don't let that remark pass without voicing your disagreement. Otherwise, your friend might think that you feel that way yourself and that you generally hold Jewish people in low esteem.

Here's another important factor in being sensitive to Jewish people and Jewish thinking: Don't confuse a Jewish person's polite interest in hearing your testimony with deep spiritual hunger. At times, Jewish people might appear to be subjectively interested in considering Christ when they are merely curious. To some Christians this has been a frustrating experience as they tried to answer a casual inquiry with intense and persuasive efforts to present the gospel. Don't be overbearing. Rather than help matters along, such untimely behavior can close the channels of communication.

Just bear in mind that centuries of persecution by some whom the Jews mistakenly identify as Christians have caused Jewish people to be defensive in varying degrees. The foremost rule for sensitivity in Jewish evangelism is to remember that most Jews are suspicious of, and defensive toward, Christianity. By being careful and loving, you can avoid offending and perhaps be instrumental in bringing your Jewish friend to see the gospel, the person of Christ and true Christianity in a different light.

CHAPTER 7

YOU THINK IT'S TRUE, BUT . . .

Some commonly held notions about witnessing to Jews are false. These erroneous ideas about Jewish people or the very nature of evangelism can lead you to deal with your contacts unrealistically and keep you from an effective witness.

THE FALLACY OF FORMULA EVANGELISM

Some people think that proper witnessing consists of following a number of precepts or principles, like so many stepping-stones along the path that leads to the pot of gold at the end of a rainbow. Unfortunately, like those who seek the proverbial pot of gold, evangelistic formula seekers may find themselves lost in the wilderness and empty-handed.

The worst feature of formula evangelism is that it often encourages manipulation in order to secure consent. Maybe some weak-minded or weak-willed individuals could be manipulated into consenting to repeat words to accept Christ, but such consent without the reality of the experience wouldn't last. As soon as they encountered opposition or enticements from another manipulator, they would fall away just as easily as they came.

Effective communication does involve a process.

The communicator must present a point and have it accepted before introducing another (i.e., it would do little good to present the Lord Jesus Christ as Savior unless the hearer first understood that everyone is a sinner before God and needs a savior).

The problem arises when we invest too much confidence in one particular method or process. That makes us insensitive and unresponsive. Then, if the process fails, we get the false notion that we are using the wrong technique or formula. We wrongly assume that all we need to do is find another formula that will then produce automatic results.

In evangelism there is not just one way of achieving results. I have been a missionary to Jewish people since 1956, and hundreds of my Jewish people have come to Christ as a result of my ministry. I certainly did not follow the same procedure with every one of them. Each person is different and must be dealt with differently.

The fallacy of using a formula was brought home to me early in my ministry. At first, I was always careful to use only the prescribed language I had been taught in a certain Jewish evangelism class. I always referred to the Savior as Y'shua Hamashiach (the Hebrew translation) rather than "Jesus Christ," and the hymnal we used in our meetings was in Yiddish, with English translations on the opposite pages. One woman was very faithful in attending our weekly meetings over a period of six months. She loved singing the Yiddishe songs, but I don't think she ever read the English translations. She even stood up in the meeting and told how much she loved Y'shua. Then one day she found out that Y'shua meant Jesus, and she never came back!

I'm not against using the name Y'shua in witnessing to Jewish people because sometimes it helps them understand the Jewishness of Jesus. However, the Jewish person must always understand that we are talking about Jesus! The point is that to rely on special Jewish language, special steps of presentation or any other method as the only "right way" is fallacious.

Would-be evangelists often feel that the key to successful evangelism must be in some magic formula. They think, "If I can be wholly dedicated to the Lord and really live for Him, if I can become thoroughly familiar with how Jewish people think, and if I can learn just the right language and the right Scriptures to quote, I'm bound to succeed every time." There is no magic formula. Even if there were, who could live up to all those things all the time?

This doesn't mean that you should be unaware of the wrong methods. You need to know them in order to avoid them. If you do a sloppy, thoughtless job, don't rely on God to fix everything. Still, it's a comfort to know that He can overrule unintentional mistakes.

I think of the testimony of one stately, elderly Jewish woman whose husband was the president of their synagogue. She came to Christ through the most clumsy witness imaginable. I was horrified to hear that she began to consider spiritual matters because a tactless Christian neighbor had approached her on the street one day and said, "You're such a nice woman; it's a shame you're going to hell because you don't believe in Jesus!" There's no worse way to begin a witness to anyone. Yet the Holy Spirit used that occasion to begin a work of grace in that woman's heart, and she was saved.

To sum it up, then, successful evangelism is not a matter of learning proper techniques. Repentance and conversion are brought about by a moving of the Holy Spirit. This book might present certain formulas, but they are only a few of many that could be suggested. The real keys to success in Jewish evangelism are a willing spirit and much patience. We must proclaim the message to many, that a few might be saved.

THE FALLACY OF LOVE

One of the most common fallacies among witnessing Christians is that all we must do is show enough love and we will win that person to Christ. Jewish people, in particular, need to see this love from Christians, for the history of Jewish-Christian relationships has been written in blood and punctuated with violence. There has been enough of an unloving attitude toward Jews on the part of the apparent Church-at-large to cause a deep-seated resentment in the Jewish community against non-Jews. At best, a feeling exists that "they (the Gentiles) don't understand us Jews and don't care enough to try."

Still, love alone is not the answer. Extending love for the purpose of evangelizing a people is not love at all, but merely bait. Love that has qualifications is just a posture and a pose. As a Christian, you must be willing to show Jewish people that you love them as persons, whether or not they ever believe in Christ. The Jewish people need your love in actions, not just words.

A common misconception is that "love conquers all." We can't love people to Christ. Even when we show Christian love, not all Gentiles will believe, nor will all Jews come to Christ. After all, God showed His love to the infinite degree at Calvary. If His love has not obtained uniform and consistent results in the hearts of inconsistent humanity, why should ours?

In evangelism a mere display of Christian love is not enough because turning to Christ violates what Jewish people would construe as their own personal integrity.

Given the fact that traditional Judaism has nothing to do with Jesus, Jews generally feel that even to contemplate accepting Christ is to plot spiritual treason. They would feel as disloyal as a child who, if it were at all possible, would choose to change parents. If that child were raised in a neglectful home that didn't meet his or her needs or supply the needed appreciation, approval and acceptance, the child would be in dire straits. Nevertheless, if neighbors expressed willingness to take that child into their family, it would not necessarily mean that the child could accept their offer. The child might feel duty bound to remain with his or her parents. So it is with a Jewish person confronted by Christian love. Sometimes that offer of love from another source, particularly if it's deeply needed, will only create inner conflict.

Frequently the secular community uses the word "love" or declares "love" in order to achieve a desired response. In reality, "love" conditioned on response is not love, but seduction. Real love is given graciously, whether or not the object of that love responds.

Thoughtful Christians will not covet souls, Jewish or otherwise. They will want to relate to others as concerned people. They will not be spiritual scalp hunters, going after souls for the glory of God. Rather they will want to be faithful witnesses. Their love will not be bait, but genuine concern. They will preach Christ because they know He is God's way for Jews and Gentiles. They will continue preaching in love, even if there is no apparent response to their message.

THE FALLACY OF IMPACT

In evangelical circles we often speak in terms of "gospel impact." Impact, in a physical sense, often causes pain and sometimes injury. In the past, thoughtless Christians have approached Jewish people without properly appraising their message or their contacts' capacity to receive it. Often the Church is talking at the Jewish people instead of talking to them.

The difference is obvious. Think of the gospel message as a baseball. If you throw a ball at someone, you set your aim, velocity, and trajectory for impact. The person's most logical reaction would be to duck in order to avoid getting hit! On the other hand, when you throw a ball to a person, you set the aim, velocity and trajectory so that the individual can reach out and grasp it. There is a difference between impact and contact.

If you want to be successful in witnessing to Jewish people, you must preach the message of God's love and redemption to them, not at them. To carry the analogy further, you must prepare to be involved in "the game" through prayer and conditioning of your spiritual muscles. You must be able to discern whether or not the other person is willing to be on the receiving end, and you must use the proper equipment. You can't play baseball with a golf club, or tennis with a volley ball.

Be sure your contact is agreeable to being on the receiving end, and adapt your message to language that the Jewish person can readily understand and with which he or she can identify.

Above all, don't push people faster than they want to go. Show love and understanding, don't rely on any one method or approach, but do be mindful of areas of offense.

CHAPTER 8

WHERE IS THE JEWISH COMMUNITY?

If the aim of our gospel ball is to the Jewish community, we must first define "community." Just about every Christian who has attended church for any length of time has heard a sermon or at least a short admonition on "witnessing to our own community." That does refer to a geographic location or a specific neighborhood, but here we will be using "community" in a broader sense.

At one time, Christians who wanted to witness to Jewish people knew that they could find a specific part of town where most of the Jews lived and direct their efforts there. Today Jewish people live everywhere. The ghetto days are over, and even if some Jews tend to concentrate in certain neighborhoods, many others do not. As a witnessing Christian, you must understand this wider view of what actually comprises the Jewish community.

No Christians are part of the Jewish community, even if they live in a "Jewish" neighborhood. On the other hand, many Jews who do not live in a Jewish neighborhood are part of the Jewish community.

"Community" is not the same as "neighborhood."

There are social and psychological elements that bind Jews together. Jewish people may live in entirely different parts of a city and seldom, if ever, see one another; yet, as Jews, they are part of the same community.

Several elements comprise the Jewish community. They are commonality, constitution, communication, culture, communion and commitment.

COMMONALITY

In this way only, some Christians live in a Jewish community. Commonality is the sharing of the same residential area, schools, civil services and commercial enterprises. It is the only element of the Jewish community that is ever shared by non-Jews.

CONSTITUTION

This involves the entity-establishing institutions that serve to separate Jews from other people and identify them together. The Jewish community is constituted to be together. Jews identify with a plethora of organizations. More than just the synagogues or temples, these organizations include Jewish community centers, Jewish free-loan societies, Jewish counseling services, Jewish relief organizations, Jewish social clubs and the like. These organizations are constituted to reinforce the Jewish identity.

COMMUNICATION

In every country where they live or settle, Jews speak or learn to speak that country's language, but words vary in connotation. As mentioned earlier, words such as "cross" or "church" that bring forth a positive emotional response from Christians do not mean the same to Jews. (Christians regard the cross as the symbol of God's love; Jews see it as an often-raised symbol of hostility.)

A zealous Christian once tried to talk to her Jewish neighbor. Her speech was effusive and filled with devotional adjectives. In describing what the Savior had done for her, she kept referring to "our blessed Lord Jesus Christ." In exasperation, the Jewish woman finally responded, "Let's get one thing straight. To you, he's your blessed Lord, but to me, he's not! He's yours, not mine; don't include me in the 'our.' Second, he's not blessed as far as I'm concerned. Even your people use his name as a swear word, and he hasn't brought anything but anguish to the Jews. Third, he's not 'Lord' to me. We Jews believe in one Lord, and it's not Jesus. Fourth, he's not 'Christ' to me. If I really believed in my own Jewish religion, I would believe that the Messiah is still to come, and you believe that he already came. To me, he's simply 'Jesus'!"

To illustrate further, Christians speak warmly of evangelism as the Church's main endeavor; Jews use the word "proselytism," which has a negative connotation. Jews like to be considered "worldly" because to them it means the same as "erudite" or "wise." Christians don't want to be called "worldly" because to them it means "unspiritual."

It's not only in theological language that Jews and Christians fail to communicate. On the surface, values appear to be the same. Yet to my people their Jewishness has a whole significance of its own. Being Jewish is a complete experience that is beyond Gentile understanding and cannot be communicated. It might best be likened to the Christian experience in Christ that is difficult to describe to anyone who has never been born again.

It's no secret that, for the most part, the Church talks

to itself in a language it accepts. Yet if Christians want to talk meaningfully to Jewish people about Christ, they must understand the meaning of the Jewish experience. Until the Church can communicate within that framework, much of its talking will continue to be at the Jewish people instead of to them.

CULTURE

The Jewish community has its own culture, as does every community. Christians often fail to recognize that their own cultural frame of reference differs a great deal from Jewish cultural patterns. Much of the Jewish culture of Jesus' time continues to exist in contemporary Judaism, but the Church has moved away from its Judaic roots. In preparing to witness to Jewish people by learning about Jewish culture, you will find additional blessing. You will gain a new perspective on the Jewish Jesus and His earthly life.

COMMUNION

Here this does not refer to the Lord's Supper but to the feeling of shared existence with others. Jewish communion is the sense that we partake of a common earthly destiny. This feeling embraces racial memories of past persecutions as well as concern for present perils and future problems of our people. It includes fellow Jews all over the world and especially the State of Israel.

To a Jew, almost every issue has a Jewish side. The anecdote is told of a man emerging from the subway in a Jewish neighborhood. Amazed and puzzled to see people running past him in apparent terror, he grabbed one of them and asked, "What's happening?" "Let me go," begged the man, "there's a lion loose in the streets. I've got to get away!" But the newcomer to the panic held fast. "Tell me," he implored, "is this good or bad for us Jews?"

Jews recognize that they share a common destiny. Hitler proved that it wasn't the Jewish religion that mattered, but our peoplehood; and if the hand of God had not intervened, our common destiny would have been total annihilation. Each Jew communes with the others, knowing that all, regardless of philosophy or social standing, share the fate of being Jews in a world that often has been hostile to them.

COMMITMENT

Each Jew has a commitment to remain Jewish. Without this element, even a person who is born a Jew will always be outside of the Jewish community. Many of us who are Jews who believe in Jesus are not allowed to be part of the Jewish community, even though we maintain this commitment.

Maintaining the Jewish identity is the most crucial issue in Jewish evangelism. Jews who don't believe in Jesus want to say that those who do have forsaken their commitment to Judaism. As construed by most Jews, such commitment means to accept the destiny, to continue in the culture and share the benefits of and responsibilities for, Jewish institutions. Jews may interpret this commitment in a variety of ways, but each one feels a sense of imperative to maintain his or her Jewish identity.

Christians don't live in a Jewish community, nor could they. So, if you want to reach "the Jewish community," remember this: You don't witness to the Jewish community; you witness to members of the Jewish community. In order to do that, you must lovingly apply yourself to the skills of communication—and that's what this book is all about.

CHAPTER 9

GET MOTIVATED

REGARD WITNESSING
AS YOUR CHRISTIAN DUTY

Jesus told His disciples, "You shall be witnesses. . . ." For those who are committed Christians, telling others about Jesus is an integral part of our personalities, not just an occasional thing. The Lord doesn't want us to wait for a special circumstance to get motivated to witness—such as acquiring an unbelieving friend or an unbelieving relative by marriage. He wants us to build our entire lives directed toward telling everyone possible about Him and praying for their salvation.

Sometimes small talk with those who are lost and need Jesus can be a sin when we consider that we have been entrusted with life and death issues to bring to them. We need to be available to them through prayer and words of consolation, and we should be prepared to raise questions in their minds that God wants to answer. That is our Christian duty.

Some people grudgingly take on certain tasks out of a sense of duty. They moan while paying their bills, grumble while paying their taxes and sigh in martyrdom as they allow an elderly or inexperienced driver to poke along ahead of them on the highway. Others perform the same duties without resentment. They joyfully write a check to the credit company, happily fill out their tax forms and gladly wait for others who are slow or handicapped.

It will help you to witness for the Lord if you understand the differences between duty, sincerity and enthusiasm. You know that witnessing is your Christian duty, but you will not always feel the same way about fulfilling it. Sometimes you will feel exuberant about telling others about Christ; at other times, you may not feel like telling anyone about anything.

This can be a problem if you feel, as many Christians do, that you must do everything out of a pure heart. If you wait to witness until you "feel right" about it, that can be a stumbling block to witnessing at all. Usually those who encounter this problem spend too much time examining their motives rather than just doing their duty. You must pay your taxes and your bills whether you resent it or feel good about it! The same is true of witnessing.

Accept the fact that you will probably feel a bit clumsy at first when you witness. That is only natural. It's as natural as nervousness before a first date, apprehension about going to a new school or jitters before starting a new job. All new experiences carry the potential for making us feel awkward—but who stays in the sixth grade because of a fear of entering junior high school? We accept the "butterflies" and dive into our new experiences.

It helps to begin evangelizing with great expectations. In *How to Give Away Your Faith,* Paul E. Little wrote:

> Every person I have known who has been used of God in personal evangelism has had an attitude of expectancy to discover interested people. In any group of people or in conversation with any particular individual he asks himself the question, "Lord, is this one in

whom you are working?" and then, as the Spirit gives opportunity, he proceeds to see what the response is.[3]

You don't know how people will respond. So, remember that we don't preach ourselves or our worthiness, but Jesus Christ—for He is worthy. 2 Corinthians 4:7 makes this clear: "But we have this treasure in earthen vessels, that the excellence of the power may be of God and not of us." Confidence in witnessing comes first in knowing that you're right in your actions, then it grows as you act in a responsible and reasonable way.

After the initial apprehension, people usually feel a certain amount of satisfaction that they've done the right thing in witnessing, no matter how the other person responds.

ALWAYS BE READY TO WITNESS

In 2 Timothy 4:2 Paul wrote, "Preach the word! Be ready in season and out of season." You should always be ready to speak for the Lord, and sometimes you can witness without even saying a word. There will be encounters that you can turn into occasions to witness; there will be times to seek an opportunity to witness and, perhaps just as important, there will be times when you can actually make an appointment to witness. The following will help you understand how to witness to everyone—whether they are Jewish or Gentile.

OUT-FRONT IDENTITY

The first kind of witness involves "out-front" identity. Even before political correctness became a

3 Paul E. Little, *How to Give Away Your Faith* (Downers Grove, Illinois: Inter-Varsity Press, 1966), 36.

popular issue, out-front religious identity was considered socially incorrect. Today's society is constantly telling everyone to keep their religious beliefs to themselves and voice them only to those who already share the same convictions. However, society is not our authority if we belong to Jesus. We Christians have a great commission from Him. He warned His followers that some people would despise them for His name's sake. As with everything else Jesus said, I have found that to be very true. Nevertheless, I believe in and practice the out-front identity method of witnessing.

The license plate on my car says, "4 Y'shua," and I have various buttons and pins that identify me as a believer in Jesus. People are surprised to hear me say that I'm an introvert, a quiet person who doesn't like drawing attention to myself. I do, however, like to draw attention to my Savior, and in order to do that, I must struggle to overcome my natural tendency toward reticence. Bumper stickers, lapel pins, T-shirts and anything that out-front helps one declare the Lord are of special help to reticent people like me. Those devices get others asking questions that God wants to answer.

Remember that in witnessing your duty is not to persuade, but to proclaim. The secret is to not take yourself so seriously or let people shame you into inaction.

Here's a case in point: One day I walked into a jewelry shop wearing a bright blue button with "Jews for Jesus" on it in white letters. The button, a little larger than a quarter, was pinned to the lapel of my coat. A clerk approached me, noticed the button and, with a withering stare exclaimed, "How dare you wear something like that in here?" Deciding to play her game, I responded, "What? You don't like my clothes?" "It's that!" she said, pointing to the button. I said, "Oh, it's my button you don't like? I wear that wherever I go. I didn't just wear it here." She said, "Well, it's disgusting." "Does that mean you're not going to sell me a battery for my watch?" I asked. She replied, "I'll sell you anything you want if you take that off." I said, "I'll take it off—if you will tell the next person who walks in that something they're wearing disgusts you and ask them to take it off. I don't care what it is." She did a double take and said, "I couldn't do that." I said, "Then stop and think. Suppose someone came in here wearing a Jews for Jesus T-shirt without an undershirt and you said they must take it off or you wouldn't do business with them. What would embarrass you more, the 'Jews for Jesus' on their T-shirt or if they stood in your store bare to the waist?"

Suddenly the clerk broke out in a smile and said, "I guess that was a knee jerk reaction wasn't it?" I said, "Yes, but it wasn't uncommon." It wasn't long before she was asking me why I believed in Jesus. Then she asked for some literature. I went out to my car, got some and handed it to her. She even gave me a 10% discount on the watch battery! In this kind of out-front witness, be patient with a person's anger and just don't take yourself too seriously. When you're out-front, some will try to shame you into silence, but keep remembering Romans 1:16: "I am not ashamed of the gospel of Christ."

ORDINARY ENCOUNTERS

Use ordinary encounters to witness with or without some identifying mark. Witnessing is affirming the truth and affirming God to others, not getting them to affirm what you're saying. A great way of witnessing is just to bless people as you come and go. For example, at a grocery checkout counter I've said to a clerk with a warm and gracious smile, "May God always give you good reason to continue smiling"; to a person with a frown, "May God lift your spirits today and give you cause to enjoy what you're doing." Upon saying good-bye to a business person, I often say, "May God give you peace now and ever more." I've noticed that people seem particularly touched by benedictions. Try this approach, and after a while it will get to be a habit.

WITNESSING BY APPOINTMENT

Witnessing by appointment is the best way. A planned visit allows for more preparation and provides an advantageous atmosphere for a meaningful discussion. You don't have to be a minister or a missionary to make a witnessing appointment. I used this approach long before I became a missionary. In my pre-ministry days, I was a salesman, and I knew the value of proper timing. A good salesperson waits for the proper circumstances to present his or her product, and this technique can be applied to witnessing as well.

The witnessing appointment can be a conversation on the telephone or in person. It can be in an individual's home or over coffee in a restaurant. Whatever the setting, it needs to be a place where your friend can move into a listening-hearing-learning mode and where you can establish yourself as the teacher and him or her as the student.

So, when someone asks you a spiritual question, resist giving an "off-the-cuff" answer and try to arrange an appointment instead. You can say, "I think I can answer that now, but could we get together again? I want to check up on something and give you a fuller, more comprehensive answer." Then ask, "Do you have a Bible?" If the person says yes, ask, "Well, will you have it with you when we get together? That's where I get most of my answers."

The best kind of witnessing appointment takes place over an open Bible. In this way you have gained at least a modicum of respect for what you have to say even before you begin. Even if a person doesn't believe the Bible, he or she will know that you do, and will listen more intently.

Before the appointment, prepare a little Bible study that points out what you've found. Think through, even rehearse, what you will say and how you will say it. Ask some Christian friends to pray for you. Then be certain to arrive for the appointment on time. Punctuality shows the serious nature of your endeavor.

Don't take much time for small talk. Open with a short prayer. Ask God to be present and to reveal Himself to your friend. Usually even a committed atheist will respectfully lower his or her gaze during such a prayer. Move as quickly as you can to the Bible.

Whatever your friend's question and your answer might be, close by saying, "Now, that's the answer I would give you because I feel that I've been born again and filled with God's Spirit. My answer might not make sense to you unless you have had the same experience." Then if you feel that the time is appropriate, add, "If God is beckoning you to come to Him, here's the way you do it. . . ."

DIVINELY APPOINTED EVENTS

Beside the out-front and ordinary encounters, there are divine encounters orchestrated by God. Back in 1966 while traveling cross-country late at night, I stopped at a convenience store. As I was about to get back into my car, I felt something being poked at my back. Though I'd never felt anything like it before, I knew it was a knife. Then I heard a gruff voice demand, "Give me your money or your life." I reached for my wallet, turned and faced my assailant and said, "You can have my money, but you couldn't take my life. My life belongs to God, and even if you killed me, I'd go to be with Him—but what about you?" He was just a teenager. Shocked, stunned and amazed, he dropped his aggressive stance and asked, "Are you a Baptist?" He confessed that he had never done anything like this before and was being "egged on" by friends who wanted him to get the money to spend on immoral purposes. He had grown up in a Christian home. The next thing I knew, he was sitting in the car beside me, crying, fearing the God who had just stopped him from doing a terrible thing. I led him in a prayer of repentance, but I was too sleepy to get his name or address as I usually would. I arrived at my destination and went to sleep. When I awoke the next morning, I wasn't sure if the incident had happened or if I had dreamed it—until I went to my car. There on the front seat was a folded up switchblade knife. I never saw the young man again, but I have always felt that the incident was a divine appointment that was a turning point in his life.

A SPECIAL LEADING NEEDED TO WITNESS?

Specially ordained witnessing circumstances may be as bizarre as my convenience store encounter or far less extraordinary. God may just move you to telephone or visit someone, and a meaningful spiritual discussion will take place. When you have that kind of unexplainable urge and you follow that prompting of the Spirit, more often than not God has also been moving in the heart of the other person to seek from you what He has given you to deliver.

Some say that they look for a special kind of leading every time before witnessing, but I don't know if that's right. As already stated in Chapter 1, Jesus told His followers to witness. Once He tells us to do or to avoid doing something, we don't need a special communication from the Holy Spirit every time to prompt our obedience. To me, that means witnessing whenever and wherever an opportunity arises. The next chapter of this book, "Witnessing On the Way," will tell you how to do that.

CHAPTER 10

WITNESSING ON THE WAY

THE WOW APPROACH

You can approach every relationship or interaction as a witnessing opportunity. To put out a conversation handle, try what I call the "WOW" (Witnessing On the Way) approach. The WOW approach always has you saying something appropriate in a given situation that can lead to a conversation about spiritual matters.

Y'shua used this approach. Consider the John 4 account of His encounter with the Samaritan woman at the well. He asked her for a drink of water. She taunted Him about the prejudice of Jews against Samaritans. He responded with "If you knew who was asking you for water, you would ask Him instead, and He would give you rivers of living water." She mocked Him with, "Well, why don't you just go ahead and give me this water so that I don't have to come here anymore?" Jesus didn't flinch. Instead, He used her glib exchange as a catapult into a serious talk about her spiritual life. You, too, can pitch off-handed but meaningful remarks that interested people can grasp as conversational handles. Here are a few examples:

- You pick up your dry cleaning or laundry. Try saying, "That's a good job, but nothing is as clean as Jesus can make your soul."

81

- Someone stops you and asks for directions. You can give the directions, then smile and say, "If you're also looking for the way to God, Jesus said, 'I am the Way, the Truth and the Life.'"
- A person relates a bit of gossip about someone or decries some criminal act in the headlines. You can respond with, "The Bible tells the truth when it says that all have sinned and come short of the glory of God."
- An acquaintance invites you out to dinner and asks which restaurant you prefer. You can say, "I'm going to be eating the Bread of Life and drinking the Living Waters for all eternity. You choose where we eat tonight."
- A gas station attendant is servicing your car. You can say, "God's power is through the Holy Spirit, and He can fill you in an instant."

This "WOW" approach will undoubtedly surprise people. It isn't typical, mundane conversation, nor is it the characteristic hellfire-and-brimstone kind of evangelism they might expect. Individuals will usually respond in one of three ways to such an approach.

1. They will be unwilling to talk about such things, so they will smile and go on as though you haven't said what you have;
2. They will say that they also believe in Christ;
3. They will enter into a discussion with you.

Even if they taunt or tease you, be sure to end the exchange with a smile. If nothing else, your Christian courtesy will leave a good impression.

The "WOW" approach is not persuasion. It's merely a Godward direction and an invitation to talk about spiritual matters. While the WOW approach works well with casual acquaintances, you can be bolder with a friend, neighbor or family member. A direct challenge will get the person's attention and usually evoke a response. Nevertheless, with the Witnessing On the Way approach, you are sowing gospel seed.

THE SEED FAITH PRINCIPLE OF WITNESSING

The key to successful witnessing is volume effort. We must witness to many to see a few come to the Lord. What would you think of a would-be farmer who goes to the seed store and buys one seed (or the smallest amount available)? When the seed merchant asks "Why so little?" the would-be farmer replies, "I want to test the seed and see how it grows before I do much work." He takes one seed, puts it in the ground, waters it, waits for it to sprout, fertilizes it and tends its growth. Even if he does that very effectively, by the time he knows whether or not the seed is productive, the growing season will be past. Silly? Yes, but some Christians witness that way. They won't invest themselves in witnessing to many or in sowing much gospel seed.

Many who try to witness become quickly discontented when they don't achieve immediate results. Their disappointment leads to discouragement, and they stop trying. The most frequent witnessing disappointments involve planned encounters that fail to take place.

If you merely hope for, or even plan, witnessing encounters with unbelievers but fail to verbalize your intentions to them, you may be rebuffed. Don't be afraid to tell people that you would like to talk to them about God. If you don't tell them in advance, you risk two disappointments. The encounter may never take place because the person doesn't know how important it is to you, or it may be aborted by the person's refusal to discuss spiritual matters. Nevertheless, don't be discouraged. Because you have prayed for that person, the witness you hoped for may come to him or her from some other Christian.

When Christians become disappointed in their witnessing efforts, it's often because they never invite the other person to participate in planning the encounter they envision. You don't get people to sit down and talk about spiritual matters by merely wishing it to happen. You must seek them out and negotiate a mutually acceptable time and place. Even then, maybe you'll ask someone to lunch hoping for an opportunity to witness, and the person won't let you steer the discussion to godly matters. Maybe you'll invite someone to your home for a spiritual discussion, and the person will cancel at the last minute.

Here's an important lesson for the would-be witness about those kinds of disappointments: Our human disappointments are often God's appointments, and those divine appointments are never disappointments.

By innumerable small events and episodes we call coincidences, God who arranges all things can—and does—impress the hearts of those He wants to win to Himself. In light of that, your expectations concerning your witnessing efforts should always rest not on your planning or presentation but on the power of God. Your hope should center on the certainty of Scripture. 2 Peter 3:9 tells us that God is not willing for anyone to perish, but that everyone should come to a repentant faith that will culminate in salvation.

You can ward off potential witnessing disappointments by understanding the parable of the sower in Matthew 13. Here Jesus uses the metaphor of the field, the farmer and the seed and the obstacles that often keep the seed from sprouting, growing and bearing fruit. Among other things, this parable tells us that though many seeds are sown, only a few will grow and bear fruit.

In the conversion process God often uses many believers and many situations to make impressions on one individual. Those impressions are then energized through the kind of faithful prayer that moves mountains and rips blindfolds from unbelievers' eyes. At best, the most we can usually hope for is just a small role in what God may be doing in an individual's life. Yet many Christians who try to witness seem to find this truth hard to accept. Remember that conversion is God's work! He's the One who sends the spirit of repentance and renewal to people.

As we sow the gospel seed, certainly we should have confidence in its quality. God guarantees it to sprout and grow. It is not stale or sterile, but even under ideal growing conditions, not all of it will bear fruit. Some of it will get eaten by birds, some will not be positioned deeply enough in the soil to grow and some will sprout, yet wither and die under the sun's heat. Nevertheless, if we sow much seed in the field, He promises that there will be much return.

Even if we sow a great deal of seed, we won't run out of it. The more we sow, the more we'll have. The more we have, the more we'll continue to plant. The more we plant, the more will grow. Best of all, the gospel is a perennial crop. Once a crop has successfully grown, it will reseed itself as others join in the planting.

Faith doesn't require you to believe that every seed you plant will sprout, grow and bear fruit. Faith only requires the confidence that if you sow enough seed, there will be a harvest in God's field. He wants you to witness, but He Himself accomplishes the actual soul winning. If you are obedient and patient, He will use you.

Don't allow yourself to become disappointed if the first seeds you plant don't sprout and grow. It just may mean that you need to be sowing more seed or that the seed you have sown needs a longer time to germinate. All that seed has a sprouting, growing and fruition appointment with God. Those of us who have witnessed over the years have encountered some who have resisted the Word of God or entirely refused to even listen. Some were even blistered when they understood what we were saying. Yet much to our surprise and joy, we often found out much later that through other means, those resisters did finally come to faith in Y'shua.

MANY IMPRESSIONS

Though our human nature wants us to be the principle agent in another's conversion, God seldom grants us that role. He is constantly reaching out through the Holy Spirit, wooing unbelievers, making small impressions and creating questions in their minds and hearts that He wants to answer. We have found time and time again that a person was impressed by words spoken at a funeral, by a tract, by a verse on a Christmas card, by music like Handel's Messiah or by a few phrases from a street preacher who to them did not appear to be all that fanatical and even seemed to make sense. Those impressions are gospel seeds. Each person's heart is a field for the seed. Though a heart may be hardened, it's not an impossible receptacle. We all know the phenomenon of granite that over many years becomes split by one seed lodged in a crevice that sprouts and grows into a flourishing tree. That knowledge should spur you on to patience and perseverance in witnessing. It should provide hope for your efforts that will dissipate disappointment. In light of that, here's an appropriate prayer as you witness to many:

Lord, please send more seed to fall on the heart of my friend, that he/she might take many impressions of you. Open his/her heart and mind, that the gospel seed You are sowing through so many of your servants might take root.

CHAPTER 11

GET IN STARTING POSITION

For many who would like to share their faith, particularly with a Jewish person, the big problem seems to be: Where and how do I begin? Once you've made the approach and your conversation is pointed toward spiritual matters, things become easier. Here are are some pointers to help you get started.

WITNESS ONLY TO "FRIENDS"

You probably would not react warmly to a stranger who began a conversation with intimate questions. Neither would most people. They usually consider religion a personal matter, not to be discussed lightly with strangers.

Before you can witness to Jewish people or to any others, you need to get them to open up to you so that you can communicate with them about important matters. You need to relate to them in such a way that they will be willing to talk to you about issues like sin and salvation. Then you can tell them the burden of your heart—that everyone needs the Lord.

Make it a policy to talk about serious spiritual matters only to people with whom you have at least begun a friendly association. As little as five minutes of pleasant conversation can be the beginning of a lasting friendship.

Don't be too eager; you can't catch a fish until it nibbles. If the person resists being steered into a conversation about spiritual matters, don't give up. An opportunity may arise the next time. Just be sure to leave a door open for future contact.

DECLARE YOURSELF EARLY

Let people know right away that you believe in Jesus as Messiah and Savior, and that you intend to tell them about Him. To fly under a false flag is wrong. As a Jewish believer, I also mention my Jewishness at the outset of a budding relationship. If people don't want to be friends with me because I'm Jewish, they don't have to. Likewise, if they don't want to be friends with me because I'm an evangelical Christian, they don't have to.

Don't crave acceptance so much that you water down your message. That leaves the person to whom you want to witness with a fuzzy image of who Christ is.

You need to make clear your intent to evangelize. If you allow people to think that you will not witness to them, it diminishes their perceived value of a relationship with Jesus Christ.

It's better that people think of you as a friendly "fanatic" who seeks every opportunity to bring Christ into a conversation than a friendly person who just happens to believe in Jesus. Will such eagerness to share the gospel isolate you from others? No. I have found that such a stance actually draws unbelievers.

FIND OUT IF THE PERSON IS JEWISH

In talking to new acquaintances you think are Jewish, you might begin by asking if they are Gentile. A Jewish person won't mind saying "No," and then there are no alternatives. On the other hand, the question "Are you Jewish?" may set a Jewish person on guard against you. Jewish people may respond defensively to such a direct question because they are often singled out for unfavorable attention by anti-Semites.

Here's a case in point: When I was nine years old, I decided, in the spirit of adventure, to explore beyond my own very Jewish neighborhood. I walked a mile or so past all the familiar landmarks until I found three boys about my age, digging in an empty lot. It looked like they were having fun making a cave, so I edged closer and closer, hoping they would see me and invite me to join them. After a few minutes, they did notice me. One of them set down his spade and said, "Hi, do you live around here?"

I shook my head. "Uh-uh, I'm just taking a walk."

"Where do you go to school? Do you go to Ashland?" he asked.

"No," I replied. "I go to Cheltenham."

"Where do you live?" he asked. I told him my address. By then he had walked closer to me. He cocked his head and raised an eyebrow. "That's over in Jew-Town, isn't it?"

I was bewildered because I had never heard my neighborhood described that way before. While I was puzzling over how to answer that, another of the boys shouted out, "Are you Jewish?"

I didn't have to puzzle over that one. "Yeah, I am." My tone must have represented what I was thinking: 'Sure, isn't everyone around here?"

Upon hearing I was Jewish, the second boy came over and spat in my face. "We don't like Jews, and we don't want any of you coming around. Get out of here!" Then there was pushing and shoving and kicking from all three to emphasize the point. I decided that discretion was the better part of valor, and since I was outnumbered, I made a hasty retreat. They pelted me with clods of dirt until I was out of their range.

After that, I stayed in my own neighborhood, and if anyone asked me, "Are you Jewish?" I always responded, "Why do you want to know?"

HOW TO BEGIN A FRIENDSHIP

You might wonder, "How can I form a real friendship with a Jewish person?" It shouldn't be any harder than making friends with a Gentile. Show by your conversation and actions that you like and are interested in him or her as a person. One good gesture of friendship is to send greeting cards at Jewish holiday times like Passover, the Jewish New Year and Hanukkah. Your Jewish friend will greatly appreciate the fact that you respect his or her religious orientation.

Seek out common interests, such as hobbies, employment or neighborhood activities as a basis of conversation. Most people are usually pleased to talk about their families, achievements, interests or hobbies. Encourage your Jewish friend to talk, and when he or she does, be a good listener. Even if you get to do only ten percent of the talking, that's okay. It's not how much you say, but what you say that counts.

Be an observer. People signal you about themselves by the clothes they wear, the cars they drive and the objects they have in their homes. The styles and colors people choose and the decorations, pictures and objects with which they surround themselves will all tell you something about them.

AFFIRM YOUR FRIENDSHIP

After a new friend acknowledges through your tactful inquiry that he or she is Jewish, affirm the person's Jewishness.

The first person who witnessed to me aroused my curiosity by saying, "I'm so glad to meet you! Every Jewish person I meet helps to increase my faith in God and the Bible, and that He is real and keeps His promises." Imagine my surprise to hear that from a Gentile at a bus stop. I had always thought that Christians considered the existence of us Jews an insult to their religion.

If you can make such an affirming statement, your friend will be equally amazed and will ask you to explain. Then you can relate how God has made certain promises about the Jewish people and Israel, and that as you see these things coming to pass, it bolsters your confidence in the truth of the whole Bible.

Later, as you get into a witnessing conversation, you will need to reaffirm that your statements to that person about the gospel are predicated upon your awareness of his or her Jewishness. Otherwise, the person will listen politely, then say, "What you are saying is very nice for you, but it doesn't apply to me because I'm Jewish."

MOVE ON TO SACRED TOPICS

Once you've passed the hurdles of initiating a friendship and of letting the person know that you are a Christian and that you know that he or she is Jewish, your next challenge is how to move the discussion from secular to sacred topics. Often the fear of clouding a cordial relationship keeps Christians from sharing their faith with their Jewish friends. Although it is possible to destroy a friendship by arguments over religion, this need not be the case. Never get into a heated argument even if you know you are right. No one has ever convinced another in anger. Just be careful to approach the matter in a positive way and respect the dignity of the individual.

Remember that God commanded us to confess Christ before men, not to convert them. If we are faithful to our task, He will cause the seeds we sow to flourish and bear fruit. Most Jewish people will admire your strong personal faith and will not be offended if you tell them what Christ has done for you.

If you have known the person for a number of years, your task will be easier because he or she will know you enough to feel some trust and respect your viewpoint. In any case, when discussing spiritual matters, do establish or reiterate at the outset of the conversation that you know the person is Jewish and that what you are saying is based on that knowledge.

BEGINNING A CONVERSATION

In talking to a friend, neighbor or family member, a direct challenge will gain attention and usually evoke a response. You can say something serious such as, "Because of who I am and what I believe, I feel that I have a religious duty toward God and toward you. I believe that in order to obey God, I need to try to persuade you to consider Him, to consider the Scriptures and to come to Christ—but I don't know how to begin. If you were I, how would you talk to someone such as yourself about the Bible and Christ?"

It's important not to say anything more than that until the person answers. Sometimes a moment of silence will pass as the person processes your challenge and tries to fit it into the framework of personal experience. Never be embarrassed by a person's thoughtful reflection after a probing question.

The person may respond, "It's impossible" or "It would be offensive to me." Accept that answer and don't press the point. You can't drill holes in a rock to plant gospel seed, but you can pray.

When you can't talk to a person about God at a particular moment, you can still talk to God about that person. Prayer does make a difference in preparing hearts to receive the gospel message. (A good case in point is Ceil's story in Chapter 5.)

Wait for the right moment to reintroduce the subject. If the right moment never seems to come, keep praying. Realize that God can use your initial offer to that person as a dormant seed that may bear fruit many years later.

On the other hand, the person may respond, "All right, I see that you feel you must explain your beliefs to me because it's your religious duty. I will listen to what you have to say."

Ask the person for a half hour of his or her time. That is long enough to cover what you need to say, but not so long as to be grinding. Make an appointment to meet with the person and talk later. Don't jump into explaining the gospel at the moment the individual agrees to talk about it.

A witnessing situation can arise out of a casual encounter. However, it's best to communicate the substance and importance of conversion at a separate time that can become a holy moment of receptivity. The person must be able to move into the mode of respectful listening as you change from ordinary conversation to holy explanation.

Consider a man courting a woman. What if he said, "Maybe next Tuesday night we could go to a movie. There are several that I would like to see. How is your friend Janie from college? Will you marry me? Maybe we could have the wedding in six months. One of the movies I would like to see is 'Gone With the Wind.'

Maybe Janie would like to come along. Do you think she would like to be in the wedding party?"

Why would anyone propose marriage in the middle of a mundane conversation? A serious suitor would structure the situation and rehearse the dialogue. He might invite the woman to dinner, bring flowers and surprise her with a ring. He would certainly create a special time and make it a memorably different occasion because the question is so important.

Likewise, how can we discuss how a person will spend eternity in the same way we talk about the latest football scores or fashion designs? When we begin to lead a person to Christ, we make an overture to the most serious matter in life. Witnessing is proposing. We propose to a person on behalf of God. Want to know more? Read on.

CHAPTER 12

PRACTICAL WITNESSING

I had just spoken to a youth group at the University Bible Church in Westwood, California. It was a great opportunity for me because many students from the University of California at Los Angeles came. Afterwards I felt hurried because I was soon to speak at the regular evening service as well, but I dutifully stood by the door to greet those who were leaving.

A pert redhead confronted me. She said that she was Jewish and did not believe any of what I had said about Jesus. Then she launched a tirade about how He couldn't possibly be the Messiah and I couldn't possibly be Jewish. It was a difficult situation because the hallway was narrow and the people behind her really wanted to leave. I raised my hand to interrupt her and said, "Look, I'd like to hear everything you have to say, but I should be greeting these people. It's the custom for a minister to stand at the door and shake hands with those who are leaving." I reached out, took her hand and said, "But I'll tell you what. I don't live very far away. Why don't you come tomorrow afternoon at 2:00 P.M. and I will hear all that you want to tell me." I handed her a business card and repeated, "I'll be at this address at 2:00 P.M."

One of the heartbreaks in missionary work among

the Jews is that we set up many appointments and often people just don't show up, but I was not disappointed. The next day she didn't come at 2:00— she came at 1:30! And from the time I greeted her at the door, she didn't stop talking.

I could only gesture her toward a couch and take a seat myself. It would be impossible to remember everything she said because her rate of speech was so rapid that I couldn't deal with all of it. It boiled down to the fact that she couldn't possibly believe in Jesus because she couldn't believe in the supernatural in this scientific age. Things like the earth being created in six days, the flood of Noah's time, the parting of the Red Sea, etc., couldn't have happened. I was astounded that she knew of so many supernatural events recorded in Scripture. Her words and sentences came in rapid fire succession without as much as a pause to reload, and I wondered if she had discovered some new way of breathing, since she never seemed to stop for air. That went on for more than five minutes, until it came to me how I could interrupt her long enough to interact with her. I was sitting on a couch at a 90° angle to her, and between us was a corner table with my Bible on it. Her eyes never left my face as she talked, so I reached a hand toward my Bible and moved it slowly until it fell off the edge with a thump. Then I bent over rather slowly to pick it up and came up talking because she had finally paused in her speech.

I think I startled her by saying, "Of course you're right! The whole case for Christianity stands or falls on miracles, and there's one miracle which, if disproved, would cause the whole case of the gospel to collapse. How did you get here? Did you drive or did you take the bus?"

I had changed the subject to see if she was really

interested. I knew she was when she responded just as immediately, as though it were all one sentence, "I drove—what miracle is that?" At that point, I began to explain the meaning of the Resurrection, and she listened. Eventually, the young woman did receive the Lord, and she became part of the University Bible Church where I had first met her.

A FEW HELPFUL SUGGESTIONS FOR WITNESSING

1. Usually it's easier and preferable to witness to someone of the same sex—man to man, woman to woman. This may not always be possible if you have a burden for a specific friend, co-worker or professional in your life.

2. It's best to talk one-on-one, privately, without the presence of other members of the family or other Jewish friends. If you are witnessing to someone of the opposite sex, you will need to balance privacy with decorum. Talk to such contacts in public places such as restaurants, parks or fitness centers rather than in your home or theirs.

3. Don't give people too much spiritual food for thought all at once. They might get spiritual indigestion. Always leave them wanting more.

4. Keep up the conversation only as long as people seem interested, or else you will become a bore. A good way to find out if people are still interested in what you are saying is to change the subject as I did with the girl in Westwood. If they are getting bored or uncomfortable, this provides a graceful way out. If they are still interested, they will bring you back to the topic at hand.

5. Always be courteous and respect the wishes of

those to whom you are speaking. Be careful not to contradict statements you regard as untruth or misinformation. Instead, say something like, "Yes, I can see how you/the Jewish leaders/the Jewish community might understand it like that."

6. Easy does it. Smile in response to the other person's statements and nod your head to affirm that your friend is important.

CONVERSATION TECHNIQUES

Conversation techniques are devices that enable us to communicate with others. They form a connection between people and truth.

1. Lay the Groundwork For a Conversation.

Salute the person. The word salutation is related to the word salubrious, which pertains to good health, good feelings or good will. With your opening words show kindness and concern. Express interest in the person's health, work situation or family.

2. Identify Yourself.

Early in the conversation let the person know that you are a Christian and that God is important to you. If the person already knows, remind him or her by briefly mentioning how God has answered some recent need in your life. It could be as simple a statement as "I'm so glad that I didn't keep you waiting. I thought I was going to be late because it's so hard to park around here, but I prayed for a spot before I left, and God answered my prayer. Someone was pulling out just as I got here."

3. Ask Leading Questions.

The best way to engage someone's mind with yours is to ask a sympathetic question and be genuinely interested in the answer. The right kind of question will lead your Jewish friend to contemplate specific ideas that you want to discuss. Don't ask questions that allow yes or no answers. Instead, ask about your friend's opinions. That will encourage him or her to talk.

Begin by asking a question that will give the other person an opportunity to reflect on your serious intentions and help you move to a serious note early in the conversation.

Good Questions
to Open a Conversation

- Do you attend a synagogue near here? (If possible, specify one that you know of in the neighborhood.)

- Would you tell me a little about the services in the synagogue? How might they differ from a church service? (If your friend has never been to a church service, that might raise his/her curiosity.)

- Can you tell me about this next Jewish holiday I have read about? Or can you tell me about the Jewish holiday that just passed?

- What are the distinctions between the various Jewish denominations?

Be interested in and sympathetic to Jewish problems and causes. Read widely enough to be conversant about matters of interest to the Jewish people.

General questions to ask about Jews and their contemporary problems:

- How does an American Jew look at Israel? Do some Jews think that the restoration of Israel as a homeland for the Jewish people is prophesied in the Bible? Many Christians believe that it is.

- Do you think that the establishment and continued

existence of the state of Israel against great odds indicates that God is actively working in Israel's history?

- How do Jewish people today feel about intermarriage?

- What are the obligations of a Jewish person to God? To other Jews?

When you feel secure enough with the person, you might try some politely pointed questions:

- Do you think it's possible to establish a unity of Jews and Gentiles?   How would that best be accomplished?

- Have Jewish people changed their thinking much with regard to the person of Jesus Christ?

- I am a person who speaks to many others regarding matters of Christ and the Church.   If you as an individual Jewish person wanted all Christians to know one thing about Jews, what would you tell them?

- Recently I heard that a number of young Jewish people are believing in Christ and that there is a movement called Jews for Jesus.   I understand that most Jews disapprove.   Can you tell me about their feelings?

Good witnessing should be a dialogue. If you engage your friend in a stimulating conversation, he or she will be thinking about those things that the two of you discussed. Encourage the person to ask a question in order that you might answer it with something that you want to say. That's the method the Lord Jesus often used.

4. Avoid Conversation Stoppers.

In the course of your conversation, use a few lighteners.   For example, if you are in someone's home, don't point out a picture on the wall and say, "Oh, I like that picture." That is a conversation stopper. Instead say, "I was looking at that picture on your wall and it caught my attention. You've lived with that painting. Why do you suppose the artist used such dark tones in depicting Moses? Do you think that has a special significance?"

Always be specific, and always ask questions that can be answered by opinions rather than by a yes or no. The question about the painting is a rester in the middle of a conversation.

5. Get the Person Talking About the Bible.

You might say, "Let me ask you this. You seem to know that I am serious about God. One of the things that brought me to that point was reading the Bible. Have you read the Bible? Do you own a Bible?" If you're in the person's home, you can ask, "Is it nearby?" (Later, in discussing Scripture, use the person's own Bible whenever possible because that's the Bible he or she will trust.)

Talk about that particular Bible. Often when you open someone's Bible, an inscription will indicate that it was given on a special occasion such as a bar/bat mitzvah or a wedding. Reflect on the individual's personal history. Recognize aloud that at the time the Bible was acquired, its owner may have been especially tender toward spiritual matters. That will often move the conversation in the direction you want it to go.

The person will comment either positively or negatively about the Bible. Then say, "I appreciate your open-minded attitude" (or if the converse is true, "I understand your skepticism, but. . ."). "Let me tell you about this Bible. If you knew what was in here and what it could mean for you, you would want to spend hours reading it. Most wise people received wisdom from knowing God. Really, did you ever stop to think about how much it matters whether or not you believe in God?"

Now you are into your conversation and should have the person's full attention.

For more sample conversations, see Appendix I at the back of this book.

CHAPTER 13

BUILDING A CASE BY CONSTRUCTIVE ARGUMENT

It is the rare Jewish person who doesn't enjoy a good argument! Most Gentiles think they should avoid "argument" for fear of offending. That's because polite Anglo-Saxon society makes no distinctions between the terms "argument" and "quarrel." But in Jewish culture, an argument is like a game of chess that you play to win. A better word than argument is "debate." A Jewish person's willingness to debate is an encouraging sign. It might mean that your friend is not completely convinced that he or she has the final answer to the needs of his or her inner life. You should realize, however, that the person will not capitulate easily. You must play the game earnestly in order to win.

ORDERLY DISPUTE IS A JEWISH TRADITION

Pilpul is a Jewish tradition of teaching that establishes facts through orderly dispute. The Talmud records much pilpul between the ancient rabbis, where questions were raised that, to an outsider, would seem like quibbling. In the Socratic method the teacher asks questions of the student; in pilpul, one teacher questions another who has stated a precept. Then the first teacher tells the second that his answer is wrong because. . . . Pilpul is gracious debate that allows for more than one answer.

To understand pilpul, consider the following story: A Gentile came to a rabbi and declared that he wanted to study "the way the Jews do" so that he might understand the Jewish people. The rabbi tried to dissuade him by telling him that he could never understand, but the Gentile was insistent. Finally the rabbi agreed to give him an oral test.

He said, "I will ask you some questions to see if you can logically come to the right answers. Two men fell down a chimney. One was dirty and the other was clean. Which one washed?"

"The dirty one, of course," replied the Gentile.

"Wrong!" exclaimed the rabbi. "The dirty one looked at the clean one and thought to himself, Amazing! We didn't get dirty by falling down the chimney. But the clean man saw the dirty one, presumed that they were both dirty, and immediately went to wash up."

The Gentile smiled. "Oh, I see."

"No, you don't," said the rabbi. "Let me ask you the second question: Two men fell down a chimney; one was clean and the other. . . ."

The Gentile was puzzled. "You already asked me that question," he said.

"No," contended the rabbi. "The other one was dirty. Which one washed?"

"The clean one," said the Gentile.

"Wrong again," said the rabbi. "It was the dirty one. He looked at the clean man and said to himself, 'It's amazing that he should fall down the chimney and remain clean,' whereupon he looked at his own hands and realized that he was dirty, and went and washed. And now, for my third question. Two men fell down a chimney; one was dirty and the other was clean. Which one went and washed?"

The perplexed Gentile shrugged. "I don't know whether to say it was the dirty one or the clean one."

"Neither!" said the rabbi. "The whole question is ridiculous! How can two men fall down a chimney together, and one come out dirty and the other come out clean?"

In pilpul, it is not uncommon for the teacher to contradict his own basic proposition. I have often used pilpul tactics in witnessing to fellow Jews. When I was teaching a Bible class on the campus of the University of California at Berkeley, Jewish students frequently wandered in to these unofficial sessions. On one occasion, a Jewish student challenged Christianity by saying, "How can you believe in the Trinity?" I asked if he knew what the word "infinite" meant. "Certainly," he said. "It means immeasurable or uncountable."

I took a piece of chalk and drew the symbol for infinity on the blackboard. "Now," I said, "according to Jewish belief and what you maintain, how many Gods are there?"

"One," he replied and recited in Hebrew: "Shema, Yisroel, Adonai Elohenu, Adonai Echad [Hear, O Israel, the Lord our God is One Lord]."

"Only one?" I asked.

He was emphatic. "Only one!"

I walked over to the blackboard again and drew the

numeral 1. "I just counted God," I said. "How can you say that He is infinite? There is the number on the blackboard." He knit his brow in confusion.

I went on: "If you say that God is but One, I will declare that He is Three; if you say that I said He is Three, then I will tell you that He is only One. Belief in the Trinity is necessary for me to know that God is truly infinite!"[4]

In Aristotelian logic, which doesn't allow for contradictions, that would not make sense, but in pilpul, it does.

DISCUSSION DESPITE DISAGREEMENT

What, then, is the difference between discordant argument and constructive debate? It's the willingness to continue to discuss a subject where there is disagreement. You say what you have to say and listen to what the other person says, and you know when and where to stop.

How to Present an Opposing Viewpoint:

1. Before you enter into a constructive argument or debate, be sure of the facts and logic of your case.
2. Carefully analyze your case and eliminate everything you are inclined to say that wouldn't help to prove your point.
3. Don't state the obvious.
4. Don't use your strongest argument of proof first. You might need it for a clincher.
5. Always understate your case rather than overstate it.
6. Rather than argue as to whether something is true, demonstrate that it could be true.

---

[4]For more on explaining the Trinity, see Chapter 17, page 146.

7. Never interrupt your friend as he or she is stating a case.

8. If you don't completely understand what kind of argument your friend is setting forth, ask questions until you do.

9. You can usually refute an opponent's argument by moving from generalities to particulars. That is, insist on primary evidence that will validate his or her evidence.

10. Offer documentation of whatever you allege, and make the other person do the same.

11. After you have stated your case, don't try to get your friend to admit verbally that you are right. Be gracious and allow him to "save face."

12. Always close on a friendly note, and tell your friend how much you enjoy discussing these things with her/him.

After any witnessing discussion, make a note of the subjects you discussed so that you may have a basis for future contact and conversation.

CHAPTER 14

TELL IT LIKE IT IS

Now you have formed a friendly relationship with your Jewish contact. You have shown by word and deed that you appreciate her or him as a person. Your friend knows that you are interested in the Jews as the people of God, that you believe the whole Bible to be God's truth and revelation to all humanity and that you want to share with him or her what God has done in your own life. How can you be sure that in your discussions with this Jewish person you are operating on the same wavelength?

TEACH THROUGH A JEWISH FRAME OF REFERENCE

If you want to engage a person's mind, it helps to be aware of and use the Law of Apperception. You need to teach the unknown and/or rejected through the known and accepted. In the context of Jewish evangelism, that means teaching Christian concepts through a Jewish frame of reference.

Before you can do that, you may need to change some of your own perspectives. For example, what about your personal concept of Jesus? Do you picture Him as the Jewish Messiah, born to olive-skinned Mediterranean people? Or do you see Him as the blond, blue-eyed Savior who (as painted by Da Vinci) ate fish instead of Passover lamb at the Last Supper and might have felt uneasy at a synagogue service? To be effective in witnessing to Jews, you must learn to think of Jesus as He really was: the Semitic-looking Jewish Messiah who spoke mainly to Jews in Jewish surroundings in a very Jewish frame of reference.

BE FAMILIAR WITH APPROPRIATE SCRIPTURE

You will need to become somewhat familiar with Jewish customs and traditions. You should also familiarize yourself with the Old Testament passages that speak of the Messiah and be sure that you clearly understand their application before you try to use them with your Jewish friends. But don't despair. It's not as daunting as you may think! This book is designed to help you do all of that. In Appendix 2 at the back of this book we have listed many prophetic Old Testament passages and the New Testament truths they portray. Nevertheless, as important as these Old Testament portions are, we need to add a new consideration here.

For a long time, missionaries to the Jews advocated what I now believe to be a wrong approach to personal evangelistic Bible studies. We were taught that the best way to speak to a Jewish person about the Scriptures was to begin with the Old Testament, particularly messianic prophecy. While we must not diminish the value of prophecy, a statistical motivational survey that Jews for Jesus conducted in 1972 indicated that only 5% of the Jewish believers we contacted were motivated toward faith by reading messianic prophecy. This statistical percentage was confirmed in 1989 at a conference at Asilomar, California, when only 7 out of 115 Jewish believers in Y'shua indicated that they had been moved toward faith by Old Testament messianic prophecies. A discussion that followed revealed that most of those Jewish believers had been influenced by the depiction of Y'shua (Jesus) either by the witness of someone or by reading the New Testament for themselves.

A NEW STRATEGY

Based on the statistics in that motivational survey, Jews for Jesus has begun a new strategy. It's so new that you probably won't find it in any other materials on Jewish evangelism. Yet it's so simple you may wonder why no one ever thought of it before. We have been using the gospel of John, both in discipling new believers and in speaking to unbelievers about Jesus.

Jesus said, "And I, if I am lifted up from the earth, will draw all peoples to Myself" (John 12:32). While those words were an immediate reference to Calvary, we can also apply them here in the broader sense of presenting His person and ministry to those who so desperately need Him. In witnessing to Jewish people, we discovered that in many cases we just had to show them the love, wisdom and person of Jesus from the New Testament. Confronted by His great Calvary love, many hearts made tender by the Holy Spirit were drawn to Christ.

It works because for Jewish people, the stumbling block is not the person of Jesus but the ingrained idea that to consider Him constitutes ethnic treason. If Jewish people can allow themselves to get beyond this obstacle, Jesus the person is irresistibly attractive. He is beyond fault. His words that ring so true and His manner as recorded in the Gospels are very Jewish. The gospel accounts were written by Jews, so a Jewish person, knowing what is Jewish and what is not, might be more comfortable with the Jewish Jesus than you think.

Of course, to help present the case to Jewish

people, you will still sometimes want to use Old Testament prophecies and their fulfillments. The best approach is to find a balance between the two.

FALSE ASSUMPTIONS

Some of the difficulty in presenting the gospel to Jewish people involves false assumptions on their part. You must, in effect, reeducate their thinking along certain lines. For example, most Jewish people are surprised to learn that Gentiles must convert to Christianity. They know that being born into a Jewish family made them Jewish, so they assume that a person born into a Gentile family is automatically born a Christian. Jewish people need to understand that while a Jew is Jewish by birth, no one is born a Christian except by being "born again."

Another false assumption involves the word "convert." For most Jewish people it has a negative valence. They think that it means to change one's religion. Show your Jewish friend (from Isaiah 6:10) that to convert really means "to turn back" to God. The Hebrew *shuv* is the root from which Judaism itself gains its doctrine of repentance *(t'shuvah)*.

FOUNDATIONAL CHRISTIAN DOCTRINES THAT WILL NEED CLARIFICATION

There is other doctrinal terminology that you will also need to explain:

Sin

A Jewish person usually thinks of sin in terms of wrong deeds. You will need to explain sin as a characteristic of all humanity. Show that the Hebrew word for sin, *chatah,* means to fall short, as when an arrow shot from a bow lacks power to reach its mark.

(We find the same concept in the Greek *amartano* of Romans 3:23 in which Paul says "all have sinned and fallen short of the glory of God.") Demonstrate that the result of human sin is separation from a holy God. Sin (the cause) and separation (the effect) keep us from being able to know or serve God as we should.

Salvation

The actual words "salvation" and "resurrection of the dead" are both included in the Thirteen Principles of Faith found in the traditional Jewish *siddur* (prayer book). Nevertheless, most modern Jewish people don't believe in heaven and hell, so they would naturally ask, "What is there for me to be saved from?"

At some point you will need to discuss judgment and eternal destiny. But rather than go into a lengthy discussion on the reality of heaven and hell at the outset, you can begin by describing our human need for salvation as a way of escape. We must be freed from our imperfections before we can arrive at a position of acceptance before the perfect and righteous Ruler of the universe.

Stress salvation as God's power that enables the arrows of our lives to reach their mark. Emphasize salvation as the victory in day-to-day living that God offers to those who accept His way of escape from their sinful selves.

Savior

Even with the foregoing explanation of salvation, the word Savior is foreign to the Jewish mind. The concept of a Messiah is much more common in Jewish thinking, but even then, many modern Jews don't think of the Messiah as a real person, as did their ancestors. Instead, they think of a messianic Utopian age when

God will bring peace and prosperity.

Try to teach your Jewish friend that Jesus, God's Messiah (Anointed One), is adequate to save from sin. Stress the fact that Jesus is our Sin-bearer and that recognizing and personally receiving Him is what really counts if we want a proper relationship with God.

CHAPTER 15

HOW TO DO THINGS BY THE BOOK

Once you have made contact and initiated a testimony by sharing with your Jewish friend what God has done in your life, you need a source of authority that goes beyond your own experience in dealing with eternal matters—the Word of God. Proper use of the Scriptures is a skill to be acquired. Many use the sword of the Spirit (Hebrews 4:12) as though it were a club. We are not to clobber a person on the head with the Scriptures. Rather, we are to present them in such a way as to pierce a heart that has been made tender by the Holy Spirit.

The Word of God cannot be used as a magic incantation with which to achieve instant results. Chances are that your Jewish friend may not agree with you on the matter of accepting the Bible as God's Word. Many modern Jews have never been taught to regard the Scriptures in that way. Your friend may see the Bible as merely allegorical writings, folk tales or a wise guide to living devised by the ancient Hebrews for the sake of perpetuating themselves as a people.

MAKE IT BELIEVABLE

How do you witness to a person who does not accept the validity of the Scriptures? Begin by demonstrating the uniqueness of the Bible.

Give a personal testimony as to how you have found the Bible to be true in your own life: "The Bible describes the nature of all humanity, and I have found this to be more accurate than any other book written. I have found that scriptural solutions to human problems are workable where human resources and solutions have failed. I have received Christ and the Holy Spirit in the way that the Bible teaches, and have found Them to be real."

Point out that the very existence of the Jewish people is a fulfillment of biblical prophecy, thus indicating that there is a superhuman power at work, revealing Himself through the Scriptures. Demonstrate that there are multitudes of fulfilled prophecies throughout the Scriptures; that modern archaeology is continually making new discoveries that affirm the historical accuracy of the Bible; that the scientific accuracy of the Bible is coming to light, as in the case of the health factor involved with the dietary laws and the agricultural principles prescribed in the Old Testament (Leviticus 25:1-7); that the Bible made mention of the fact that the earth is round (Isaiah 40:22) at a time when this theory was unheard of.

Remind your friend that more disagreement exists among the skeptics than among those who view the Bible as the revelation of God. Put the burden of proof upon the unbelievers. Ask them what in their experience makes them doubt the integrity of the Scriptures. Have they studied them and found them to be inaccurate?

MAKE THE SCRIPTURES AVAILABLE

Once you have succeeded in arousing your Jewish friends' interest in the Bible, hopefully they will show some desire to read it, especially the portions that speak about Christ. A word of caution is necessary here: Don't try to get people to accept a New Testament before they have been moved by the Holy Spirit to read it. If you press a Bible upon someone who is not ready to read it, the recipient may accept it out of politeness and just allow it to gather dust on his or her bookshelf.

IF A JEWISH PERSON DOESN'T HAVE A BIBLE, SHOULD YOU GIVE ONE TO HIM OR HER?

If you feel that your Jewish friend is ready to study the Bible and you really want to give one to him or her, do it, but not as a gift. It's a bit unctuous to present a Bible as a gift, because the Jewish person would regard it or any other Christian literature as a tool designed to persuade him or her of your view that Jesus is the Messiah.

When Jewish people do indicate to you that they would really be interested in reading some of the things you have been discussing, that's the right time to lend rather than give them a copy of the Scriptures. They will be far less likely to postpone reading it if they feel you may be wanting them to return it after a time.

If you feel strongly that you want to give someone a Bible, it can be given in secret as your gift to the Lord without the person knowing that you have done that. Just say that you can get a Bible at a really low price. Then go out and buy one for whatever you must pay for it and "sell" it back to the person at a deep discount. It's good to let people buy their own Bibles because if they don't care enough to do that, it's unlikely that they would value one you would give them enough to read it.

When a person does accept a Bible, you will want to check his or her progress frequently to see if he or she is really reading it. The best way to accomplish this is by asking an indirect question: "Have you come to the place in _____ where it talks about _____?"

WHICH VERSION OF THE BIBLE SHOULD YOU USE WITH A JEWISH UNBELIEVER?

Much good can be said on behalf of the modern language translations and paraphrased versions of the Bible. One of these is a new rendition by Dr. David Stern called *The Jewish New Testament.* It restores names, places and holidays mentioned in Scripture to their Hebrew or Aramaic equivalents. For example, the name Jesus is rendered Y'shua, and Paul continues to be called Shaul. It also puts certain Jewish customs and traditions into context. This version has been particularly useful to Jews who have already come to faith in Jesus.

Some prefer the *New International Version,* the *New King James Version* or the *Living Bible.* Whatever version is your favorite, remember that your Jewish friends will feel more comfortable using their own Bible if they have one. Most Jews own at least an Old Testament, and some have a Bible that contains both Old and New Testaments.

One of the first visits I ever made as a missionary was to the apartment of an elderly Jewish man in New York City. When I asked him if he had a Bible, he answered, "Oh, yes, the very best brand!" As he hurried off to get it, I wondered out loud what he meant. Then he brought it to me and said proudly, "It's a Gideon Bible. I didn't buy it. It was given to me by a friend." I was very glad he had it, but I didn't have the heart to tell him that Gideon Bibles are given free to anyone who wants them.

Another time I was visiting in a more Orthodox home where a couple had agreed to see me because their son had become a believer in Jesus. Before they would talk to me, they had talked to their rabbi. The rabbi had told them that missionaries were tricky and that we had special versions of the Bible where the texts had been perverted to make it look like the Jewish prophecies pointed to Jesus. I was a bit dismayed to hear that until the man continued, "So, I bought my own Bible, and if you think you can show me from Scripture why I should believe in Jesus, use this one." I was delighted to discover that it was a King James Version, Scofield edition!

BE CONFIDENT IN USING THE BIBLE

Many Christians are hindered in discussing the Bible with a Jewish friend by the fear that their contact's knowledge of the Old Testament is far superior to their own. If you are one who feels inadequate in this way, set your mind at ease. If you were to assume that your Jewish friend knew very little or nothing at all about the Old Testament, you would probably be closer to the truth than if you presumed the reverse. In most Jewish communities, less than half of the Jewish children receive formal religious training. Those who do receive such education are taught mostly culture, customs, liturgy, the Hebrew or Yiddish language, Jewish holidays, and Jewish history, rather than religious doctrine. If the Bible is taught at all, it is in the form of stories or is used as a textbook for learning Hebrew.

USE THESE HELPS
IN SHARING THE SCRIPTURES

The following suggestions should be of considerable help to you in sharing the Scriptures with a Jewish person.

First, a word of advice: a strange thing happens to Christians when they pull out their Bibles to witness. Suddenly they rise on invisible pulpits and their voices ring out with authority. Before you open your Bible to begin teaching someone, be sure that he or she has agreed to become your student. Likewise, before you begin preaching to them, know that they are willing to be your "congregation."

1. When referring to the Old and New Testaments together, use the term, "the whole Bible" to indicate its unity and completeness. If you refer to either Testament separately, use the terms "Hebrew Portion" or "New Testament Portion." Some Jews think that we Christians call the Jewish Bible the Old Testament because we think it's obsolete. No Jew calls the Jewish Scriptures the "Old Testament."

2. As already mentioned, when witnessing to Jewish people in their homes, use their own Bible rather than yours. You should be aware, however, that your friend's Jewish Bible will not always agree with your own translation. In Jewish homes the Masoretic text is used. It gives different translations of such messianic verses as Psalm 2:12 and Isaiah 7:14 and 9:6. This is because wherever a variant reading that gave no messianic import to the text was possible, the Jewish translators insisted that it was the correct reading; after all, they weren't about to help the evangelists prove their point. (It would probably be best to avoid discussion of

these texts if you are using the Masoretic translation.) You also will find that the Old Testament is arranged differently, with the books of First and Second Chronicles last instead of Malachi, and Daniel placed apart from the other prophets. Before you go flipping through your friend's Bible looking for a text, check the index.

3. The best way to wield the Word of God is to use it to make direct points. Don't use a "scatter gun" approach with the Bible. For years, I taught Jewish evangelism seminars and frequently went along with some of my students as an observer while they attempted to witness to their Jewish friends. Later we would discuss what they had done right and what they had done wrong. One such occasion involved a young man, also young in the faith, who was visiting his friend in the hospital after surgery. The patient smiled through his discomfort and said to my student, "If Jesus is the Messiah, why don't we have peace in the world?" My young protege quoted John 3:16 from memory, whereupon the patient said, "What does that have to do with it?" The would-be evangelist shrugged. "I don't know," he said, "but it's the Word of God, and it should speak to you!" **Use the Bible either to raise an issue or to speak to an issue. Don't just quote random verses.**

4. When citing a text, explain the context. If you quote a verse, be sure to explain any elements that the person may not understand, such as: (a) the writer of the passage; (b) the historical setting; (c) proper nouns, names of people and places.

5. When dealing with a prophetic passage, make sure that your listener is acquainted with the date of the

prophecy, so that he or she can see that it was fulfilled hundreds of years later.

6. Don't hesitate to use the New Testament portion of Scripture to illustrate a point or show a historical background.

7. Occasionally put the Bible in your friend's hand and ask him/her to read the verse aloud. It's easier to focus on something while reading it than while listening to someone else read it.

8. Don't overwhelm Jewish people by turning to many passages in quick succession. Remember that the Bible language is probably foreign to them, and they need time to understand the concepts and let them sink in slowly.

Even though your Jewish friend might not believe that the Scriptures are the inspired Word of God, don't hesitate to quote the Bible. Most skeptics are not as established in their skepticism as you are in your belief. God honors His Word, and the Holy Spirit can use the seeds that you sow.

CHAPTER 16

JOHN'S GOSPEL AND THE APOSTLES' CREED AS TEACHING TOOLS

As already stated, don't be afraid to use the New Testament in witnessing to a Jewish person. Previous missionary tradition endorsed using the Gospel of Matthew for this because Matthew supposedly wrote to a Jewish audience. After reconsidering this view, however, I concluded that Matthew was not the best source for beginning instructional and evangelistic visits. Here's why:

Whereas each of the Gospels seems to serve a different purpose, it is merely a hypothesis that Mark related to the Romans, Matthew to the Jews and Luke to the Greeks. Besides, if Matthew did write to a Jewish audience, it would have been to those who were familiar with the Temple and the Old Testament. That is not the case among modern Jewry. Jewish worship and Jewish people have changed since Bible days.

Their general religious knowledge has decreased markedly. For these reasons, it's better just to present Jewish unbelievers directly with the claims of Christ.

The Gospel of John is the clearest and most powerful way to accomplish that. It contains most of the important themes of the Old and New Testaments and gives the better overview of who Y'shua is. It presents the most detailed picture of the Savior, a higher Christology and numerous narratives that are dramatically developed. John's narratives paint a better picture of Y'shua in the various episodes of His life. John gives us more of the texture of Jesus' life. The Jesus we love is most clearly revealed and more highly exalted in this Gospel.

POINTS OF EMPHASIS IN JOHN 1-4

It is best to begin with the most difficult themes in these early chapters. Contrary to previous widely used evangelistic methods, I have come to believe from personal experience that the deity of Christ should be the first matter to be addressed rather than the last. John 1:1 immediately establishes the deity of Christ:

"In the beginning was the Word, and the Word was with God, and the Word was God."

Don't be afraid to assert that doctrine from the start. Then continue with John 1:2,3:

"He was in the beginning with God. All things were made through Him, and without Him nothing was made that was made."

This reinforces Y'shua as the Creator, and verse 4 further states that:

"In Him was life [vitality] and the life was the light of men."

The life that was in Jesus was the life of the Holy Spirit, and the Holy Spirit is the life force of the

Godhead.

John 1:6 states, "There was a man sent from God, whose name was John." This not only introduces John, but it defines a prophet as a God-sent man—someone who speaks for God, about God—who foretells and tells forth at the same time. The term "sent" in verse 6 is the same as will be later translated "Apostle." John is described as a messenger with authority. It is expected that people will receive his message and, more importantly, will receive the Lord about whom he prophesies.

John 1:7 states that John came to bear witness of the light, that all through him might believe. So, here we find that God purposes for people to believe in His Son through the witness of others. In this case the witness is through the prophet John.

The Word described by the prophet John was the true light:

"That was the true Light which gives light to every man coming into the world. He was in the world, and the world was made through Him, and the world did not know Him. He came to His own, and His own did not receive Him" (verses 9-11).

You can go back and point out from John 1:5 that the natural thing for people to do is not to accept the Lord, but to reject Him, and that the reason for this rejection stems from the fact that all humans are in darkness.

To summarize, the first eleven verses of the Gospel of John already reveal quite a bit about the major teachings of Scripture. We learn about the deity of Christ, the creation of the world, the depravity of man and the nature of faith and belief.

In presenting this portion of Scripture you can utilize the corollary Old Testament texts that speak to those issues and doctrines. When dealing with the Creation, turn to Genesis 1. When presenting the deity of Christ, turn to various messianic prophecies. After all, the entire Scriptures, both Old and New Testaments, converge in the person of Christ. It is not that the Old must be read through understanding of the New or that the New must be read in light of the Old, but that both Old and New, the entire expanse of God's progressive revelation, converge in the person of Christ.

HUMAN INIQUITY

Starting at John 1:11, and then looking over the whole book, you can show why some didn't receive Jesus, why people didn't come to the light. Point out the passage in John 3:19 that says, "And this is the condemnation, that the light has come into the world, and men loved darkness rather than light, because their deeds were evil." Link that to Romans 3:23, which says, "For all have sinned and fall short of the glory of God." Then lead the person's thought by asking, "Until now, are you one of those who haven't received Him?"

At this point, you can make sure of the person's understanding by asking questions such as, "The Bible says that Jesus was the true light that gives light to every man coming into the world. Who is that light? Well, if you look ahead, the light is the Word of God, or the logos." Then you explain, "This is what John is calling Jesus. He was in the world, and though the world was made through Him, the world did not recognize Him. He came to [that which was] His own, but His own did not receive Him." Emphasize the word, "receive" because this is what you will ask the person to do—to receive the Savior. "But as many as received Him [again emphasize the word "received"], to them He gave the right to become children of God, even to those who believe in His name."

The next verse introduces the new birth, "who were born not of blood, nor of the will of the flesh, nor of the will of man, but of God." It's important to show here that an action is required. One must receive what God has given in order to acquire it. It takes an act of the will. A person must make the choice to obey God and to appropriate what God has provided.

Then go from John 1:12 where it talks about receiving the Lord and emphasize that Christ is the sin bearer. This can be done handily from John 1:29ff where it describes Y'shua's baptism: "The next day John saw Jesus [Y'shua] coming toward him and said, 'Behold! The Lamb of God who takes away the sin of the world!'" You can link that verse to Isaiah 53:6, "All we like sheep have gone astray; we have turned, every one, to his own way; And the Lord has laid on Him the iniquity of us all."

Once you get into the term, "iniquity," use the route of telling about the lamb. Most people think that in witnessing you start by dealing with sin, talking about judgment, hell and so on. No. Instead, talk about the lamb, and the Isaiah 53:6 explanation of sin as falling short. You can link that to Romans 3:23 which teaches, "for all have sinned and fall short of the glory of God." At that point, you establish the concepts of general sinfulness and individual sinfulness.

CHRIST'S RESURRECTION

John 2:19-22 involves the Resurrection. It is also very good because the next verse (23) shows Y'shua at Jerusalem during Passover. It reinforces the Jewishness of Jesus and this is particularly good, even for non-Jews. One of the evidences for the truth of Christianity is that it came through a culture whose people are, for the most part, not believing it.

Continuing through the text, we encounter Nicodemus, a ruler of the Jews whom we must assume was a rabbi, a learned man. The first thing Nicodemus recognized about Jesus was His miracles. Here's where Jesus used the "either/or" technique. Nicodemus conceded that no one could do such signs unless God were with him. Jesus replied, "Most assuredly [in the strongest possible terms], I say to you unless one is born again, one cannot see the kingdom of God." Once again the new birth is introduced and the "either/or" comes into play. That is, either Nicodemus was "born again" and had the awareness that experience produces, or he didn't know what he was talking about. Y'shua was trying to show the Jewish leader that God wanted something more from him that he had not yet given. Here you can point out that God still wants that from us today.

You can also present John 3:12: "If I have told you earthly things and you do not believe, how will you believe if I tell you heavenly things?" In other words, we use these metaphors of the new birth because heaven is so indescribable that we must present it that way. Then you can get into other salvation passages.

Everyone who witnesses wants to get into John 3:16, and that's always a good passage. Nevertheless, a prior fact that you need to establish is that of the Resurrection. Jesus is a historical figure. No one will dispute that He lived; few will dispute that He died by crucifixion. Yet in depicting Him as Sin Bearer, it is the Resurrection that makes His offering of Himself unique. You can cross reference the fact of the Resurrection with Isaiah 53:10b: "When you make His soul an offering for sin, He shall see His seed, He shall prolong His days, and the pleasure of the Lord shall prosper in His hand." The dying victim of Isaiah 53:8 and 9 is the risen victor of Isaiah 53:10.

John 3:14-16 infers that Y'shua is the Sin Bearer. In John 3:14 the Old Testament imagery of the serpent lifted up in the wilderness does not refer to Jesus being exalted but to His atoning death. The serpent in the wilderness was a picture of God's judgment on sin, as was the cross at Calvary. Yet unless we establish the fact of the Resurrection before teaching the significance of the cross, we are left with a rather sad, hopeless conclusion. Except for the Resurrection, the death of Christ at Calvary is an ignominious tragedy, so bear that in mind.

Having established the Resurrection, you can get back to John 3:16. It says, "For God so loved the world that He gave His only begotten Son, that whoever believes in Him [the Son] should not perish but have everlasting life." You can explain it to someone this way: "The 'whoever' is the person who chooses to believe, or perhaps the better word is 'trust.' God wants you to believe in Him and trust Him, and He wants you to have the joy of belonging to Him."

It's important then to go on to John 3:17-20, which shows that the whole world is condemned already. At this point a person should be able to see and acknowledge his or her sin. I usually ask if the individual wants things to be different. I explain that in our present human condition, the world and the flesh dominate our spirit and cloud our spiritual perception, but by the New Birth we are born again with the power to see the Kingdom of God and become spiritually alive. We can then function spiritually after we confess our condition of sin, renounce it and turn to the Messiah for that new life. If a person can understand that there is a whole life he or she has not experienced because of sin and now wants to experience, that individual is ready for the next important step. We will deal with that step in another chapter.

THE APOSTLES' CREED AS A SUPPLEMENT

You can supplement the teaching of John's gospel by combining it with the Apostles' Creed, one of the oldest documents of the Christian church. The Apostles' Creed is basic to what we need to teach people at the start of their Christian walk. Your teaching of the new or near believer, therefore, becomes both didactic and catechetical. Most of the themes of the Apostles' Creed, which follows, are conveniently found in the early chapters of John's Gospel:

I believe in God, the Father Almighty, maker of heaven and earth.

And in Jesus Christ, His only Son, our Lord, who was conceived by the Holy Spirit, born of the virgin Mary, suffered under Pontius Pilate, was crucified, died and was buried.

He descended into hell.

The third day He rose again from the dead.

He ascended into heaven and sits at the right hand of God, the Father Almighty.

From thence He will come to judge the living and the dead.

I believe in the Holy Spirit, the holy Christian church, the communion of saints, the forgiveness of sins, the resurrection of the body, and life everlasting. Amen.

What more do we really have to say to new or near believers? The creed summarizes most of what we would want to teach them. If you teach through the Gospel of John, you can systematically deal with the doctrines of the Apostles' Creed within the context of the Gospel. This is not eisegesis, but sound exegesis, and the common message of the creed and the Gospel is apparent.

CHAPTER 17

OBJECTIONS— DOORS TO BE OPENED

If Jewish people are not taught anything else about religion, they are told early in life, "We Jews don't believe in Jesus. He is the God of the Gentiles." Actually, there is no official Jewish position regarding Jesus Christ except this negative statement which supports 2,000 years of unbelief. Nevertheless, Jewish people feel they must defend this tradition even though they may not understand why. In order to do this, they must raise intellectual barricades as a defense mechanism against the Christian message. Therefore, you must realize that many of the objections and questions you will encounter will be the result of preconditioning, rather than a real study of the subject that has led to sincere conviction.

Theology or doctrine is not the issue. Theological liberalism is widespread among the Jews today. The Orthodox Jew who keeps the Law is very rare. Even those men who consider themselves Orthodox think nothing of shaving their beards and doing light work on the Sabbath. Few Jewish women keep the dietary laws in their homes as did their grandparents, and only a handful of modern-day Jews retain the hope of the coming of a personal Messiah.

THE REAL OBJECTION TO CHRIST

The real and usually unspoken Jewish objection to Christ is the unwillingness to face the personal consequences of believing something that is so divisive. Faith in Christ will set Jewish people apart from the majority of their fellow Jews and label them as traitors. Confronted with the truth of Christ, many Jewish people count the cost and decide that the price is too high.

The best way to counter this problem is to voice the unspoken objection with a pointed question: "If the Bible is true, and if Jesus is the Messiah after all, are you willing to learn the truth and believe in Him, even though your decision might bring about severe personal consequences?" At this point you can remind your Jewish friend that following God was never the easy thing to do. Abraham, Moses, King David and Elijah all suffered because they chose God's way rather than the accepted norm of their day.

You must be prepared to give answers for the most common objections, but keep in mind the real issue in order to avoid disappointment and frustration. Be aware that after you have offered what you consider a logical and satisfactory explanation for a given objection, it will not necessarily follow that the person will immediately accept Christ. However, it can mean that one more barricade has been eliminated so that the pilgrim may avoid stumbling over it as he or she continues the spiritual quest.

In order to bring Jewish people to Jesus, you must reach them in their fortress of defensiveness with love and understanding so that they willingly let down the barriers. It is often a slow process over a period of months and even years. It requires much energy, patience and love before a child of Abraham is brought to the point of welcoming Jesus into his or her life.

In the meantime, we must deal with the questions and objections. It is wise to recognize that many questions regarding Christian beliefs (for example, the nature of the Trinity discussed later in this chapter) can never be fully explained to the finite mind. Nevertheless, there is no question or problem to which we cannot give a satisfactory answer if the person is seeking to believe. On the other hand, if someone is determined not to believe, no answer will be adequate. In any case, be prepared to answer all your Jewish friend's questions and objections, even though they may not be asked in complete sincerity.

The following questions and objections are some of those most frequently raised by Jewish people.

SOCIAL OBJECTIONS

1. Why do we Jews need Christ? Our morals are as good as Christian morals.

   Answer: It's not a matter of superior morals, but of coming to God in the way that He has ordained: through Jesus, the Messiah. (Quote John 14:6.)

2. Christians hate the Jews. I can't go over to the side of those who have persecuted my people down through the ages.

   Answer: A real Christian who is following the teachings of Jesus cannot hate anyone. We have great respect for the Jews because we realize that they have given us the Bible and the Messiah Himself.

3. How can we Jews believe that we are God's chosen

people, or even that there is a God, when someone like Hitler can kill six million of us?

Answer: Look at it from the other side: Six million were killed, but twelve million were left alive. If Hitler, or Haman, or the Russian Czars had had their way, there would be no Jewish people today. God has miraculously preserved the Jews through 3,800 years of history, while many other nations mentioned in the Bible (such as Edom, Babylon and Ammon) have disappeared from the face of the earth.

DOCTRINAL QUESTIONS

1. The Trinity: You Christians worship three gods, but we Jews know that God is one.

Answer #1: We Christians are not tri-theists. We do not believe that there are three gods, but rather that the entire Bible infers a plurality in the Godhead. The word for God in Genesis 1:1 is Elohim, which literally means "gods." Genesis 1:26 and Isaiah 6:8 use plural pronouns for God, and Isaiah 48:16 definitely implies plurality.

Answer #2: We believe in one God who reveals Himself in three persons. The Trinity is a mystery that we cannot understand. Comprehending the nature of God is completely beyond human ability.

While many people might not be prepared to hear you confess this lack of understanding, you could explain it like this:

Answer #3: The concept of number doesn't apply to God. He is infinite. That means immeasurable. If He were an absolute unity (yachid), as the siddur (Jewish prayer book) and many rabbis understand it, we could count God by simply drawing one tally mark. When we say that the concept of number doesn't apply to God, we also recognize that our way of perceiving God as three distinct persons—Father, Son and Holy Spirit—is only our human perception. If we think that God is one—merely one—then He shows Himself to be three; yet if we say that He is three, He is but one. These number perceptions are held in tension, so that God is neither one nor three, but infinite. Nevertheless, there are three "persons" of the Godhead who have a co-equal and co-eternal existence.

2. The Incarnation: How can a man become God, as you Christians teach?

Answer: We do not believe that a man became God, but just the opposite. God became human in order to communicate His love toward us. If God is God, then He is great enough to do anything He wants, even become a man.

3. The Virgin Birth: It is impossible to believe in a religion that teaches that a virgin can have a child.

Answer: God is supreme over His creation. He brought the laws of nature into effect, and He can suspend any of them at will to carry out His purposes. Look at the parting of the Red Sea, the stopping of the sun for Joshua, the birth of Isaac in Sarah's old age, the provision of the manna for forty years in the wilderness, and the many other miracles that God performed for the Israelites as recorded in the Bible.

4. What about the unfulfilled prophecies about the role of the Messiah? Jesus couldn't be the Messiah because He did not fulfill the prophecies that say Messiah will bring peace on earth. We still have wars.

Answer: If the Jewish people had accepted Jesus as their Messiah, He would have brought about the Kingdom of God on earth at that time. Nevertheless, the peace that Christ brings is a peace of heart that the Bible says passes all human understanding. Even while the world is at war, we who know Jesus, the Messiah, can have peace of mind and peace with one another. There cannot be real peace on earth until people have had a change of heart so as to make the Kingdom possible. Eventually this will be true when the whole nation of Israel enters into this experience of the change of heart. And the time is coming when the Messiah will return to rule on the throne of David. At that time He will establish peace throughout the world.

5. Original Sin: You Christians say that everyone is sinful from birth, but we Jews believe that all people are basically good.

Answer: We believe that the sin nature pervades the whole human race. We judge by human standards and find some to be better and others worse. The Bible describes sin as a condition of human existence that does not pertain to a particular act, but rather an attitude, which is Godlessness. The best of people, like Abraham, Moses, and King David, all committed acts of sin. The prophet Isaiah said, "All we like sheep have gone astray; we have turned, every one, to his own way" (Isaiah 53:6). That righteous prophet indicated that it is only human for each person, himself included, to want self-fulfillment rather than to fulfill the precepts of God. King David said that his sin was a condition from birth (Psalm 51:5). If sin is not universal, why is there a Day of Atonement that is universally observed among the Jewish people as the most solemn of all holidays?

6. The Need for a Mediator: We Jews go directly to God when we pray. We don't need an intermediary.

Answer: Modern Judaism does teach that there is no need for an intercessor. In this, it is different from the revealed biblical Judaism of the Torah. The Torah records that Moses was an intercessor with God on behalf of Israel, and he spoke of Another, greater than he, who would be like him, who was to come (Deuteronomy 18:15). Ancient Judaism not only required intercessors as priests, there was a place of intercession in the Temple, a means of intercession in the blood sacrifices and a day of intercession in the Day of Atonement. Modern Judaism does not have an intermediary, and this is one reason why thoughtful Jews ought to be asking whether Christ just might be the God-appointed Intercessor as described by Rabbi Paul (Shaul) in Hebrews 9:11-15.

7. Paganism: We Jews have held to certain concepts of God for 3,500 years. Christianity, which came along later, is based on a Gentile misunderstanding of the Old Testament theology and is tainted with pagan thought.

Answer: To a degree you are right; the Christian concept of biblical religion is often expressed in Gentile terms because that is the culture in which it flourished. Nevertheless, it is a Bible-centered religion. It deals with many of the themes of the original Old Testament revelation, namely the sacrificial system, which modern Judaism tends to discard as primitive superstition. Much of the Pentateuch (Torah) concerns itself with how to achieve oneness with God through the sacrifices, but modern Judaism without the emphasis on sacrifice and sacrificial atonement is a later, humanistic development. Biblical Christianity concerns itself with the ancient theme that seems to be most important in the Torah.

CHAPTER 18

PRAYER, YOUR SECRET WEAPON

People have often asked me, "Which scripture passage or which argument finally convinced you to believe in Christ?" I must say that it was neither, for when I first heard the case for believing in Christ from a Gentile friend, I was afraid that it might be true. I counted the cost of believing, and decided that I would not hear or consider anymore about it. This fellow had no encouragement from me. I made him understand that if we were to remain friends, he must stop discussing religion with me. He knew enough not to press the matter, but he didn't give up.

Instead of talking to me about God, he began to talk to God about me! Orville Freestone and his family prayed for me every day at each meal for four years, and at the end of that time, God reached me by first touching the heart of my Jewish wife. She and those faithful friends, and several others who were much encouraged by her confession of faith, then turned the big guns of prayer on me. Seven weeks later, I was convicted by the power of the Holy Spirit that the Bible is true and that Christ is real. Had they not all prayed so fervently for me, I'm sure it could have been another seven years instead of seven weeks before I received Christ, or maybe never at all!

USE INTERCESSORY PRAYER

The key to effective witnessing to anyone, Jew or Gentile, is intercessory prayer, the priestly ministry of every believer. Prayer is your secret weapon in the battle with Satan for souls. He knows that one day the Jews will be the ones to go forth and proclaim Jesus, the Messiah, to the whole world, and he will do everything in his power to hinder that. Therefore, it is particularly necessary, especially in witnessing to Jewish people, to seek God's help in overpowering the forces of darkness that are at work in this world.

If you lack the incentive to pray fervently for the lost sheep of the house of Israel, just pray that God will give you that burden. Pray for opportunities to witness and that you will have the sensitivity and wisdom to say the right thing when those opportunities present themselves.

Pray often for your Jewish friends, and mention them individually by name. Rather than just pray, "Lord, please save so-and-so," ask for specific progress—their desire to study the Bible, their willingness to speak with you about Jesus, or a softening of their hearts to some particular doctrine or Scripture passage.

Ask Others To Pray

On the other hand, a more general type of prayer is advisable when involving others to help you pray. By all means, ask the people at your church to help you pray for your Jewish friends, but don't give too many personal details or identify them by name. If you do, there is always a possibility that some well-meaning but insensitive Christian might meet one of those unbelievers sometime and blurt out, "Oh, yes, I know who you are. We have been praying at church that you would get converted!" That could engender a real setback. If you have actually been talking to the Jewish person about spiritual matters, he or she would perceive it as a betrayed confidence. Furthermore, just the negative valence of the word "converted" could be damaging because to Jews it denotes turning away from one's Jewish identity, loyalties and allegiance. (This is also discussed in Chapter 14.)

Tell Your Jewish Friends that You Are Praying for Them

In witnessing to a Jewish friend, do share as part of your testimony your personal experiences with prayer. You might tell how God has answered some specific prayers in your life, and how you have been comforted and have felt God's presence in times of crisis. This can lead to an offer to pray for some specific need or problem your friend is experiencing.

Very often a Jewish person who may not yet be receptive to your prophetic ministry of preaching the Word will accept your priestly ministry of prayer on his or her behalf. Through your witnessing the individual may sense that you have a special relationship with God and may want to share with you some problem or stress. Let the person know that you will pray for the specific matter of concern, such as an illness, a forthcoming surgery or a family crisis. However, don't mention that you are praying for the person's salvation as well. That could scare her or him away for good!

Never hesitate to say a table grace before meals when entertaining Jewish friends in your home. They will not be offended but will be impressed with the fact that God is very real to you. You could introduce the matter by saying, "In our home it is our custom to thank God for our food before we eat." However, keep it short and simple, and by all means, avoid turning it into a ten-minute sermon on theology.

Also, as a general rule, don't ask an unconverted Jewish person to pray aloud with you. Jews are accustomed to reading most of their prayers from the Jewish prayer book. Your friend would be completely unfamiliar with the extemporaneous manner of praying that Christians use and would probably be embarrassed over not knowing what to say, even if he or she had the heartfelt desire to join in.

Of course, the obvious joyful exception to the rule is when you know that your Jewish friend is ready to receive Christ. Then it will be your privilege to help him or her formulate the prayer of faith that will accomplish what you have been praying for in secret all along!

See Chapter 20 on how to be a spiritual midwife.

CHAPTER 19

BREAKING THE CHURCH BARRIER

Once friendship and communication have been established, the time might be ripe to ask your Jewish friend to visit your church with you. Don't be afraid to extend such an invitation. Frequently, unbelieving people—both Jews and Gentiles—respect the Church as an important force for moral and ethical good in the community. Maybe your Jewish friend has never been inside a church except as a wedding guest ten years back. Very likely he or she is somewhat curious as to what a real church service is. In such a case, your friend will not mind visiting your church and may even welcome the opportunity, as long as you give assurances that it is just a visit and there will be no embarrassment or pressure of any kind.

BE WILLING TO VISIT A SYNAGOGUE

Along with this invitation to visit your church, you ought to express your willingness to visit a synagogue with your Jewish friend. However, a word of caution is needed here about so-called "dialogue" between Christians and the Jewish community. All too often arrangements are made whereby the local minister and the local rabbi "swap pulpits" for a day, or address each other's congregation at some social function, all in the name of "brotherhood" and "good will" and "better understanding." The problem with this kind of exchange is that in the interests of harmony and politeness, neither side says what is really important or germane to his or her doctrinal position for fear of offending. Much back patting and hand shaking takes place. Then each party retreats to his or her own side of the ideological fence, and they have not had a real dialogue at all. Don't let this happen between you and your Jewish friend.

Real dialogue can only take place when both parties have a viewpoint to express and are willing to change some of their views to harmonize with the other's so that there is agreement. For the convinced Christian, Christ is not merely a viewpoint but a living relationship that cannot be denied. No genuine Christian is prepared to enter a dialogue that may call for an admission that Christ is anything less than "Lord of lords" and "King of kings." Likewise, only a few Jews are willing to enter into a dialogue that may call for an admission that He is. You must each be willing to acknowledge your differences and discuss them, but dialogue in the real sense is not possible.

After you have prayerfully decided that your Jewish friend is ready for a church experience, by all means extend that invitation. Your friend may delight you by saying yes the first time. Then, again, he or she may say, "No, I can't this time, but I would like to go another time." This could be a polite way of saying no, but it might be genuine. The temporary refusal could be based on a previous commitment or the untimely visit of a censorious Jewish friend or relative. So, ask again, at least once or twice, before you conclude that you are being turned down permanently.

AVOID SPECIFIC PITFALLS

When your Jewish friend does agree to visit your church, here are a few suggestions that could help you avoid some pitfalls and make it a meaningful and happy experience for both of you. Best of all, the experience could even be a stepping-stone on your friend's path to salvation.

First, find out what the program will be for the particular worship service you have selected. For example, your Jewish friend will probably react in a negative manner to a sermon on stewardship. Likewise, it is not a good idea to bring an unbelieving Jewish friend to a prayer meeting for the reasons mentioned in the previous chapter on prayer, nor to a service when Communion will be observed in which an unbelieving person cannot—indeed, should not— participate.

Church socials or seasonal musical programs are excellent services to which you can bring a Jewish friend. To break the ice of attending a Christian meeting, even better than services or functions scheduled on the church premises are home fellowship meetings or Bible studies. (However, avoid bringing an unbelieving friend to home prayer meetings where each person prays and one who didn't want to pray might feel self-conscious.)

Many churches plan annual or more frequent special programs that would be of particular interest to Jewish people, such as Christ in the Passover presentations that link Christian typology to Jewish traditions. Also, there are programs available that present Jewish Christian drama and the new Jewish Christian music, which has a distinct ethnic sound and at the same time presents a clear gospel message. Any of these would be quite appropriate. They are usually publicized in the local newspaper, which would be helpful in extending the invitation. If you have Jewish friends whom you would like to bring to such a service, you might let your pastor know and ask him to pray about scheduling a special program that would be available from Jews for Jesus or one of the other Jewish missions.

If your Jewish friend accepts your invitation to attend a specific church service, be sure to inform your minister that you will be bringing a Jewish guest. He will want to share your prayer burden, and he may be able to add to or delete something from his remarks that will be just the right thing to promote a favorable response from your friend.

PREPARE FOR YOUR FRIEND'S VISIT TO CHURCH

Plan your arrival time. If you plan to bring your Jewish friend to a regular worship service and your church participates in lengthy prayers and credal recitations with which an unsaved person could not identify or feel comfortable, it might be wise to come a bit late. In such a case, you could plan to arrive just before the sermon or special music that precedes the sermon and slip into some inconspicuous seats at the back of the sanctuary.

Be aware of the Jewish perception of church offerings. Most Jewish people are unfamiliar with church offerings because synagogues and temples are supported by annual or life membership fees and pew rentals. Before the offering is taken, tell your unbelieving friend that although the church is supported by offerings, this is not an "admission charge." Explain that the offering is an avenue of worship for those who are believers, and that your friend is your guest.

As you introduce Jewish friends to others at your church before or after the service, do not identify them as being Jewish. If you do, it might embarrass them or leave them open to the pressure of some overzealous individual who thinks he or she can lead anyone to Christ by talking long and earnestly. If you do see one of the church people applying this kind of "instant evangelism" pressure, you can interrupt by saying, "Yes, my friend and I have been talking about those very things, but perhaps right now is not the best time to continue the discussion."

Don't try to sell your Jewish friend on the superiority of your particular church or denomination. Point out that all truly Christian churches are in agreement on the important doctrines of the Bible with regard to God and humanity, yet they may differ in their form of service or organizational structure.

Don't be apologetic about anything, such as the length of the service, the small size of the building or congregation, the quality of the special music or the newness of the pastor. Why point out defects your friend may not have noticed that could make him or her critical? You want your friend to remember this experience favorably.

After the service, you may wish to entertain your friend at your home or go out for coffee where you can discuss his or her reactions in private. Hopefully the experience will open new avenues of thought about Christian attitudes and doctrine that will become another step toward your Jewish friend's willingness to accept Christ.

CHAPTER 20

HOW TO BE A SPIRITUAL MIDWIFE

God's harvest of souls is not always reaped by those who have sown, and at times we do reap where others have planted and watered the seed. Many times a Jewish person has come to me after a faithful and often lengthy witness from a Christian friend. Then after just a few moments of additional conversation with me, the person has confessed Christ by "going forward" at a church or evangelistic meeting. Whether God uses you to sow or to reap, know that if you are faithful in proclaiming God's message, He has promised: "My word . . . shall not return unto Me void, but it shall accomplish what I please, and it shall prosper in the thing for which I sent it" (Isaiah 55:11).

You have every reason to believe that if you have been faithful in your witness to many, some will want to make the decision that will bring them from death to life.

It's a high calling and a real blessing to be a spiritual "midwife" at the new birth. Nevertheless, many Christ-loving, people-loving individuals miss the blessing of leading someone through a conversion experience simply because they fear that asking for a decision will offend or be a "turnoff." If you have been witnessing to someone and feel that the time is right, don't let fear turn you away from asking that person for a commitment to Christ!

RELY ON THE HOLY SPIRIT'S LEADING

You may be wondering, "How can I know when someone is ready to make a decision for Christ?" In this, you must rely on the leading of the Holy Spirit, but one signal that the person might be ready is that he or she receives the Word of God gladly. That is, he or she studies the Bible with you, accepts it as being true and welcomes Bible answers to problems and questions.

HOW TO BEGIN

If you think the person may be ready, your next challenge will be how to introduce the subject. Use the text in John 1:12 and ask, "Are you ready to receive Him now and become His child through the new birth?" If your friend says, "No, not yet," don't press for a decision.

If, however, your friend says, "yes," you can proceed. In talking to a Jewish person, point out that in order to become a Christian, Buddhists or Hindus might have to renounce their faith and all that they believed before, but for a Jew, coming to Christ is merely coming home to the God of Abraham, Isaac and Jacob. Caution your friend that accepting Christ will not be easy. It may have serious social consequences, and certain sacrifices will be necessary in order to live a life that will be pleasing to God. At the same time, you should encourage a commitment by pointing out that God will provide the strength to overcome the

social barriers, and the Holy Spirit will empower the
new believer to live the Christian life.

If your friend agrees to make that commitment to
Christ, explain the process by using the metaphor of
marriage. Say, "The new birth is not like the first birth.
Our first birth is a natural event over which we have
no choice. The new birth is a supernatural event that
does require us to choose. In this, it is more like a
marriage than a birth. God loves you and has always
loved you, but perhaps you haven't been aware of
His love. He has wanted you to be His in the way
that a person who loves yearns for another person—
but He also wants to be yours. He wants you to
belong together! He wants to be your loving
Heavenly Father and you to be His child. As in a
marriage proposal, God now says to you: 'Will you be
mine?' He wants to know if you are willing to turn
from belonging to sin to belong to Him. In order to
do this, you must accept His offer through prayer. Are
you ready to pray now?"

Ask your friend if he or she would like help in
finding the right words to say. The answer is usually
yes. Then you can lead the person in a prayer like
the one below. You might want to keep such a
written prayer on a 3x5 card in your Bible, wallet or
handbag:

*God of Abraham, I know that I have sinned
against You, and I want to turn from my sins. I
believe that You provided Messiah Y'shua as a
once and for all atonement for me. With this
prayer, I receive Y'shua as my Savior and my
Lord. I thank You for cleansing me of sin and
making me worthy of the life You have for me
through Messiah. Amen!*

In order to make the commitment more real, the next thing you should do is to encourage your friend immediately to confess Christ to someone, preferably a sympathetic person who will be able to rejoice with him or her. It could be an interested pastor or a Jewish Christian friend. You might call that person on the telephone and say something like, "I'm here with _____, who has just made a very important decision that he/she would like to share with you."

At this time, notice the emotional state of the new Christian. If the individual seems emotionally untouched, or says, "I don't feel any different," point out that it sometimes takes a while for the realization of a spiritual commitment to sink in. Even though new believers might not feel "saved," faith has accomplished their salvation for them.

OUTLINE BASIC THINGS
FOR THE NEW BELIEVER TO DO

God's new child will need much nurturing and encouragement from you. As you give this guidance, it will be your joyful privilege to see the baby believer grow and mature as, by God's grace, he or she works out the new life which the Holy Spirit has begun.

After you have prayed with your friend and he or she has confessed Christ to someone, you should give the person some idea of what will be expected of him or her. Never imply that the Christian life is easy, but give the assurance that whatever one might need to give up for Christ's sake, God will replace it with something better. Outline some basic things that the new believer should start doing right away in order to grow.

Daily Bible Reading

Advise the new believer to read the Bible every day,

even if at first it's only for fifteen minutes at a time. Point out that as a result of the new birth that has just taken place, your friend is a babe in Christ and needs the milk of the Word in order to live and grow.

In our Jews for Jesus ministry, we have found that new believers frequently have a greater hunger for Bible study. In many instances we have arranged to meet with new Christians every day for extensive Bible reading and discussion until this voracious appetite tapers off to a slower pace. The tapering off usually occurs after several days or weeks. We also have found that the new believer has a high capacity for Bible memorization. At the outset, many will undertake to memorize as many as six Bible passages a day.

Jews for Jesus furnishes a free booklet to new believers that provides a list of Bible memory verses. The booklet also gives advice on such subjects as "How to Tell Your Family." If you need to give one of these to a new Jewish believer, it can be obtained upon written request from Jews for Jesus, 60 Haight Street, San Francisco, California, 94102-5895. E-mail: jfj@jewsforjesus.org; Web: www.jewsforjesus.org. Or you can e-mail the author of this book at MityMo@aol.com.

Daily Prayer

Advise the new believer that he or she needs to commune with God often in devotion and thanksgiving, and also to make specific requests. You can list subject matter for prayer, such as the salvation of the person's loved ones, wisdom in telling others about the person's new faith, guidance in daily life, etc.

With respect to prayer, remind the new believer that God is interested in the smallest details of our lives and wants us to ask so He can give. If your Jewish friend is still uncertain about what words to use in prayer, or what to ask for, you might introduce the Lord's Prayer as a beautiful example of how to pray. Another real aid to the prayer life of the new believer can be the standard hymnal that is still used in many churches. The traditional songs in these older hymnals usually contain very meaningful devotional thoughts and sound doctrine.

Testifying And Witnessing

Teach the new believer from Scripture that God expects us to confess our faith before others as the occasion arises. (You can use Romans 10:9,10 and Acts 1:8.) As already stated, a new believer should begin by telling at least one person immediately after receiving Christ. Then perhaps for the next few times the baby Christian may seek to tell others who will also be glad and offer encouragement. Of course, eventually we all encounter those who may not receive our message so joyfully. Your friend must be prepared for that, too. You can supply the necessary encouragement (from personal experience) that when we are faithful in witnessing, God helps us through those rough times.

Regular Fellowship With Other Believers

New Jewish believers may or may not be ready to attend church immediately. Nevertheless, they should be encouraged right from the start to go regularly to some kind of worship service, Bible study or prayer meeting. It will be helpful to introduce a new Jewish believer to any other Jewish believers you may know. Sometimes new Jewish Christians think that they are the only Jews who have ever made such a decision. They need to know there are others. The more mature Jewish believers can then be a great comfort and help to the new believer as he or she faces problems and situations they have already experienced. Read on for more about new Jewish believers and church attendance in the next chapter.

CHAPTER 21

NEW JEWISH BELIEVERS AND CHURCH MEMBERSHIP

Helping new Jewish believers settle into a worshiping congregation is almost as hard as getting Jewish unbelievers to consider the person of Christ! That's because the majority of Jewish people do not attend weekly synagogue services and are unaccustomed to the habit of regular worship. Except for holidays and special occasions, most Jewish people avoid synagogue attendance. It's not that they disapprove of the synagogue. They just don't regard it as the fountain of Jewishness, because Jewishness and Judaism are learned first at home and only secondarily at synagogue. Thus, most Jews feel no need to attend weekly services.

That, however, is only one factor in the uneasiness most Jews feel about church attendance. Every church, no matter how informal, has its own symbols and rituals. Jewish people, who have little or no church experience, may often regard these symbols and rituals as alien and quite remote from their new and simple faith in the person of Christ.

Another problem involves the new Jewish believer's potential disillusionment with nominal Christians in the church. For many nominal or merely cultural Christians (those who are weak in conviction but strong on convention), weekly church attendance is only part of a routine. To see little of Jesus in the lives and behavior of such church members can become a stumbling block for a new believer.

Another difficulty occurs when, in constructing a worship situation, churches try so hard to provide "something for everyone." Some of the currently popular contemporary services and kinetic modes of worship might trouble some Jews who were accustomed to liturgy and solemnity in the synagogue. On the other hand, another segment of Jewish people with no synagogue orientation at all might find a more solemn, deeply reverent service with slow, serious music more funereal than worshipful.

But never mind about those problems. You cannot tailor the church to the convert, but you can prepare the convert to accept the church as it is. In advising your newly believing Jewish friend about regular church attendance, the following should be of help.

WHAT TO TELL NEW JEWISH BELIEVERS ABOUT THE CHURCH

1. Not every person in the church, even some who may attend regularly, have the full assurance of salvation. Some merely go to church because it is the tradition of their family, not because they have made a firm commitment to Jesus.

2. Some church people have strange notions about Jews. At least some of the non-Jews in most church

congregations need to be educated about Jewish people. In certain geographic areas, some Gentiles may have never even met a Jewish person. Jews who attend a church should be prepared to encounter some misunderstanding from the uninformed. That kind of unawareness might even foster inappropriate comments from some non-Jews about Jewish people. Nevertheless, a Jewish person who visits or attends a church should not confuse such a lack of understanding with anti-Semitism.

Even true Christians may unknowingly hold prejudiced opinions they have heard from anti-Semitic people. They may have heard that "Jews have special abilities with money," or that "Jews control Hollywood," etc. Sometimes they accept such ideas uncritically, not realizing that they are untrue. Usually when such misguided Christians become informed, they discard their anti-Semitic notions because they are ready to love. (And here's a little aside on that subject: No True Christian would ever call a Jew a "Christ killer." First of all, true Christians know that Christ gave up His life— He said "no one takes it from me." Besides that, He rose from the dead—and no judge or jury would ever convict someone of murder when the victim was very much alive!)

3. Many new believers have a false notion that something special is supposed to happen to them as they attend worship. It is best to tell the new believer that attendance at worship is a duty, and if there is joy in it, that joy comes as a bonus. Jewish people understand the concept of religious duty better than the concept of going to worship for enjoyment. The proper attitude you should foster in them about

regularly attending worship is that they come to church to obey God. The Bible commands that we get together with other believers (Hebrews 10:25), and when we obey that command, it pleases God.

At this point, we must mention messianic congregations. There are some who maintain that all Jews who receive Y'shua should join messianic congregations that employ a Judaic expression of their faith. Such congregations are not new, but they began to proliferate in the early seventies. Over the previous hundred years, there did exist mission congregations that were attended by Jews who felt more comfortable with the "Jewish" ambience of those groups. However those congregations existed primarily to meet the needs of Jewish immigrants who did not understand the language of the more conventional congregations.

Subsequently, with a rise in the number of Jewish people coming to Christ, the newer messianic groups sprang into being because some new believers had a strong desire to preserve their Jewish identity. Some also wanted a more Jewish form of worship. As previously stated in another chapter, Jewish people often have aversions to Christian symbols such as the cross, the crèche and depictions of Jesus. At the very least, those symbols puzzle Jews, who have been taught from childhood not to make images of God. At the worst, they seem to a Jewish person to verge on idolatry. Sometimes word symbols also can be a stumbling block. To the Jewish mind, Christian means Gentile, church is equated with the persecutors of the Jews, convert means traitor, etc.

For these reasons, sometimes a messianic congregation can be very helpful in bridging the culture gap between Jewish and Gentile Christians. Nevertheless, what is good for one Jewish believer in

Jesus is not necessarily best for all Jewish believers.

We recommend that you personally visit a messianic congregation before you endorse it or take your Jewish friend to it. You will find that many are excellent, but unfortunately, others are inadequate. Worse yet, a few are heretical. Generally it can be said that messianic congregations are much like any other churches— many are good and some are not.

If your Jewish friend who is a new believer can settle more easily into a doctrinally legitimate messianic congregation, his or her presence there can be a testimony to the whole Jewish community.

On the other hand, if that new Jewish believer joined your church, he or she would be a testimony and encouragement to the Gentile Christian community in that church to witness to other Jews.

In encouraging your Jewish friend to attend church, remember to consider Jewish taste and sensitivities. Some things about church that are obvious to you need to be explained because a church service is different in many ways from a synagogue service. As previously mentioned, these differences include offerings, unison recitation of prayers, the length of the services and what is or is not considered proper decorum. The synagogue paradigm leads Jews to think that all worship is similar, but in fact, synagogue is radically different from church, and new Jewish believers need to be prepared for the differences.

To sum it up, new Jewish believers need to find their place in the Body of Christ. Nevertheless, there is a need to prepare the new Jewish believer for the Church so as to avoid culture shock.

CONCLUSION

THE FOUR B'S

In conclusion, think back to your own conversion. Even though you may have been raised in a Christian environment, your total understanding and commitment to the Lord Jesus Christ didn't happen overnight. At best, it took place as the result of many years of Christian nurture and love during your formative years—and possibly you went through a period of rebellion and doubt before becoming a real child of God. In witnessing to Jewish people, just remember that the Jewish person has years of conditioning to overcome, as well as the natural human inclination to turn away from God. Here are four short, simple reminders that can help you witness to Jewish people and to others who need the Savior:

1. Be a friend.
2. Be patient.
3. Be faithful to God's Word.
4. Be prayerful.

In days gone by, it was the rare Jewish person who would darken the door of a church or open his or her mind to consider Christian teachings. Yet today there is a new generation of Jewish people. Those who have lived in the free world have been less persecuted than their forebears. They are more informed and more broad-minded. Those who have recently come out from behind an atheistic society in the former USSR are curious about spiritual matters. Many are beginning to realize their own spiritual hunger and are finding that these spiritual needs are not being met by the rabbis or by the synagogue.

You, as an evangelical Christian, should be heartened to see the interest that individual Jews are beginning to show in the claims of Christ, and you should be preparing to speak to the growing remnant that God is calling to Himself.

APPENDIX I

SAMPLE CONVERSATIONS

Responding To Particular Situations

1. Someone says, "I really don't want to talk about religion/the Bible/Jesus."

   Say one of the following:

   A. Do you ever talk to anyone about it? Did someone else make you uneasy about it?

   B. I would feel better if you could tell me why you don't want to talk about it.

   C. Neither did I for a long time, but one day. . . (then describe your change in attitude as part of your testimony).

   D. Approach the comment as though you were conducting a survey. Say, "I know most Jewish people don't believe in Jesus, but would you mind if I asked you a couple of questions?" That kind of remark defuses potential anger, and you stand a better chance for a thoughtful response.

   E. Pause and say, "I can appreciate that. I don't think I should push you to listen, but if you don't mind, I would like to send you some literature I've found meaningful so that if there ever comes a time when you do want to know, it will help you."

2. The Gospel-Resistant Person

   This person goes a little further than the one who simply says, "I don't want to talk to you." He or she is gospel-resistant but still willing to talk with you up to a point.

183

A. Make unacceptable excuses for the individual. In other words, suggest an excuse the person would find unconscionable. Say something like, "Yes, you're right. I can understand why you wouldn't want to discuss this. After all, you don't feel qualified; you're not really a scholar." Or say, "I can understand why you don't want to know. You must feel it's wrong to go against the thinking of religious authorities you trust."

Who would admit, "I don't want to know"; "I'm too ignorant to find out"; or "I never deviate from my crowd. I'm content to be just one of the flock who goes along with the intellectual stampede"?

B. Use the salesman's method. There is a book titled, *The Sale Begins When the Customer Says No*. That author is not lying. When customers say they are not interested, it merely provides the salesperson with a real challenge.

A salesperson might respond, "I know you aren't going to buy my product, but help me understand your reasons so I can do it right the next time. Explain why this product is not usable by someone like you. I can tell you really want [a vacuum cleaner or whatever] and I need to know why this model or my presentation of it doesn't meet your needs. Would you just take a couple minutes and help me?"

Here's how that translates into witnessing. "I know you don't want to hear what I have to say about Jesus, but could you help me understand why an open-minded, articulate person such as you feels ill at ease to discuss it?"

When the person answers, don't use the reply as a tool to begin leveraging him or her into a discussion as the salesperson would. Instead say, "Oh, I see. Thank

you. You've helped me to understand." That gives
you the ability to come back another time and say, "I
thought about what you said in our last conversation.
It was very instructive to me. Do you mind if I ask you
two or three more questions?"

C. Ask leading questions, so named because they go
somewhere.

When the Person Has Already Said No, Try These Leading Questions:

1. "I know you're not going to let me talk to you about
   Jesus, but if you were to do so, what do you think
   I would say?" (In other words, "You have some idea
   of what I am going to say to which you are saying
   no. I'd like to find out what it is.")

2. "The people in your circle of friends who talk about
   Jesus—who do they say He is? Do you think that
   the information you have been given is fair and
   objective?"

3. "I know you don't want to talk about Jesus, but
   what if I were to talk about Him to your
   (father/mother/sister/brother)? Would that offend
   you? Let me tell you what I would tell [whoever you
   specified]. How do you think she'd feel about it if
   I told her that God loved her and had a wonderful
   plan for her life?"

4. "Can I ask you something? I know you don't want
   to hear about Jesus, but if all the Jewish people in
   the world changed to believing in Him, would you
   care to believe in Him then—because then He
   would be at the center of the Jewish religion?"

5. "So the way I understand it, you think the Bible is
   trash like last week's newspaper, right? You don't
   believe that the Bible should be disregarded like

trash, do you?" This question is the same as giving an unacceptable defense. It puts words in a person's mouth that will make him or her uncomfortable to leave it at that.

How to Respond to An Angry Person

1. Let angry people vent their anger. The following are samples of angry remarks you may encounter:

- "I don't believe in Jesus. I can't let myself believe. The idea of God offends me. If the Bible is true, even a little bit true, and God talks about justice and doing right, why doesn't He do right by us? If there is a God, and I'm sure there's not, He's either out of control or He doesn't care. He's disinterested, and all of the agony and pain and all of the wrongs go unnoticed. Such a God isn't worth much to me. I'd rather believe in the ants on the ground, because at least if an ant offends me I can step on it. I'd rather believe in the birds flying overhead because I can step out from under them before I get splattered. If there is a God, I'm angry with Him, and neither you nor anyone else is going to change my lifetime of experience and deprivation that makes me feel this way."

- "I've learned one thing about people in general and religious people in particular. Everyone is a hypocrite. People are all for themselves, and the Nazis were just one kind of people who were for themselves. Listen, I used to give every year to the United Jewish Appeal. Remember their old motto 'Give until it hurts'? It started hurting and I kept on giving. I wrote them that I was hurting; I was retired and I couldn't keep up with my $1,000 annual pledge on an $18,000 income. I said I would try to keep up, and the very next thing I got a form letter asking if I couldn't give more because of the Ethiopian Jews who were in need. I said to myself, they don't care for Ethiopian Jews. They don't care for this Jew. They don't care for anyone. They're in it for themselves. That's been my experience of any and every kind of religion. It's all a racket."

2. Respond to the venting. Such a soliloquy could go on anywhere from twenty minutes to an hour and a half. Let the person deal with his or her feelings. Don't you deal with them. When he or she comes up for air, just say, "It sounds like you've endured a lot of hurt. It also sounds like there hasn't been anyone who really cared. I want to tell you that I don't want anything from you. I want to give you something. I want to tell you that God cares for you. I know you don't believe in God, but could I pray for you?"

3. Try to get into the Word. Say, "I would like to leave you with a thought and a prayer. My favorite Bible verse is. . . ." Then read or recite it and pray.

4. Pray with the person: Say something like, "Lord God of Israel, [name] is in a lot of pain and I pray that you take away that pain so he/she might have some joy today." Or "Lord, I thank you for [Ed's] good health and I pray that you keep it that way. Bless him and bless his household. Show him that you care. I also want to pray for his children who are not talking to him, that they might see how much he loves them. In the name of Y'shua, amen."

5. Follow up. Send a note or a postcard. Say something like, "I hope you're enjoying the kind of peace I prayed for you when we talked." Then call in about a week and ask if the person received your note or postcard.

Tips for Getting a Conversational Response

1. Take advantage of position. Exert upon the person his or her own role and position.

If you are Jewish, you can say to a grandmother or other relative, "I need to know why you believe the way you do because you and I have a family relationship that I respect."

To a teacher you can say, "I'm sure you could teach me a great deal if I were open to learn from you. As one who knows the value of instruction, do you think you could learn something from someone else? Surely you wouldn't stand up in front of those you teach and say, 'I know everything. I have it all down.' We need to learn from one another."

2. Be a listener. In the business world, a salesperson would listen carefully to the customer's reason for saying no and then address that particular issue. For example, "Now I understand why you said no. You thought a canister vacuum has less power than an upright, but did you know that this canister has a 3/4 horse power motor, whereas an upright has only a 1/2 horse power motor?" Or, "You like uprights because they have a rug beater on the bottom, but did you know that this canister also has a rug beater and weighs only half as much?" The same applies in witnessing: "You have always

felt/have been led to think. . ., but what if. . . ," or
"Did you know that. . . ?"

3. Have humility. Behave as though everyone in the
   world had something to say to you, because often
   they do.

4. Don't "slam the door." In other words, don't let go
   entirely. Just say, "Okay, you're upset about this
   right now. Maybe I didn't put it well. Let's talk
   another time—in a few weeks, a few months, a few
   years?" Make a little joke and leave with a smile.

Sample Conversations on Commonly Expressed Subjects

1. On the Jewish religion and Jewishness:

Christian: "What do you know about the Jewish
religion? What is the Jewish religion based on?"
Contact: "I guess it's based on the Talmud."
Christian: "On what is the Talmud based?"
Contact: "The teachings of the rabbis."
Christian: "And on what do the rabbis base the
Talmud?"
Contact: "The Tenach."
Christian: "And the Tenach is called what?"
Contact: "The Bible."
Christian: "And your rabbi says that the accounts of
the Bible are not literally true, right?"
Contact: "Right."
Christian: "Your rabbi preaches a religion that
doesn't go anywhere. If it's derived from the Bible,
and he denies the Bible, what kind of Judaism is that?"

Will such a strong answer work? If you use such a
strong approach, you are obligated to give the person

something in return. You need to lift up that individual. Say, "I know your rabbi is sincere, and I know that you sincerely believe him. But did it ever occur to you that some of these reactions, conclusions and prejudices are not well thought through? Your rabbi must be a wonderful man. I'm sure that when he talks to you on other subjects where he feels less threatened, he tells you, 'Why don't you think for yourself and come to your own conclusions?' Since he can't tell you that about Jesus because it's such a sensitive subject, let me say it."

2. On knowing one's Jewish identity:

Christian: "How do you know you're Jewish?"

Contact: "Because my father was Jewish."

Christian: "And how did he know he was Jewish?"

Contact: "His father told him."

Christian: "And how did he know he was Jewish?"

Contact: "From his father. Every male in my family had a Jewish father."

Christian: "How did they all know they were Jewish?"

Contact: "I guess it goes back to the very beginning when people decided to be Jews instead of Goyim (Gentiles)."

Christian: "And who was the first Jew?"

Contact: "I don't know. Who was the first Jew?"

Christian: "I think we can find that answer in the Bible. Abraham was the first Jew."

Contact: "Is that what it says in the Bible?"

Christian: "Do you want to look at it? We could look at it together."

Contact: "Okay."

Christian, after reading or quoting Genesis 12:2: "If

that's the basis for knowing whether or not a person is Jewish, the Bible has other things to say that are true as well. . . ."

3. On a person's disappointment in God:

A person may ask, "Why should I believe in a God who disappoints me?"

You can reply, "Do you realize what you're saying with a question like that? Stop and think. You're basing God's existence on whether or not you believe in Him. What you really mean is you're not going to serve Him if you don't like Him."

4. On the Holocaust:

Some people say, "I could never serve a God who allowed the Holocaust."

You can say, "The Holocaust shows that God gives us freedom. He allows us to do as we please even though sometimes we choose evil. You might say that the Holocaust poses a problem for all people. How could man be so cruel? Why did God allow it? Who knows why God made an elephant with long ears and a long trunk? Who knows the mind of God and what motivates Him? Why does He allow one thing and not another? You don't have to be a Bible reader to know that all of this is beyond us. All of these questions are meaningless. We can't say that God does or does not exist because of the Holocaust. Either He is or He isn't. His existence doesn't depend on a historical event."

Another sample conversation on the Holocaust:

Contact: "I'm not going to serve Him if He was the God who allowed the Holocaust. That's for sure. What could you say that would make me want to serve such a God?"

Christian: "What could I say to make you want to serve God? Do I know what motivates you? Why don't you tell me some of the things that motivate you. What could move you to go through a great deal of trouble and modify your life?"

Contact: "I could serve a worthy cause, but a God who would allow the Holocaust isn't worthy; He's evil."

Christian: "You know what the Holocaust shows? It shows the love of God. God loves humanity so much that He's even given us free will to defy Him."

Contact: "I think we have two different world views. I know you're a religious person, but how could you possibly equate the Holocaust with God's love?"

Christian: "You didn't hear my point. Sometimes something seems to be one thing when it is something else. Did you ever hear a wife or a husband say, 'Honey, do you think we should stay so late?' When you hear the prefix 'honey' used in a certain tone, it's more than a suggestion. It's an imperative. Sometimes words used in a certain way mean the exact opposite by compensation. Let me tell you how the Holocaust proves God's love. You probably won't accept it. I don't expect you to accept it, but you can get a glimmer of a very different world view. God loves man so much that he will let us do as we choose, even if what we choose is evil."

5. On the character of God:

Contact: "But if He's a God who allows His creatures to do that, He's an evil God. A good God would never allow people to do that kind of thing."

Christian: "Well, did God make evil people?"

Contact: "God made everything, like you just told me. If God made everything, then He made evil people."

Christian: "When did God make people evil? The Bible says that in the beginning, God made everything good. Good deteriorated and became something else. Listen. Once in a while I like to put some cream in my coffee. Sometimes the cream curdles. Do you know why? Because it deteriorates with time."

Contact: "So we deteriorate with time?"

Christian: "Morality deteriorates with time. Are people better today than they were 100 years ago?"

Contact: "I don't know. I'm 87, not 100."

Christian: "One thing we find is that a loving God lets us be what we choose to be, even if we are evil. He even lets you say that you won't believe in Him and you won't serve Him if He's the God of the Holocaust."

Contact: "Ultimately, if you're one of those born-again Christians, you're going to tell me that I can believe what I want until the very end when the same evil God who allowed the Holocaust will throw me into hell along with all the people who killed six million Jews. How can I believe in a God who you say is going to put me in the same place with Hitler?"

Christian: "Easy. Not only you, not only Hitler, but most of humanity will be sent there. When you call God evil, you're calling yourself good. Either you're with Him or against Him. You've already said that He's evil. He doesn't like the idea. He says, 'Fine. Go do what you want, be what you want for now, but I'm still the God of eternity.'"

Contact: "I still say that if God allowed the Holocaust, then yes, I'm better than God because I would never have allowed that to happen if I were God."

Christian: "That's right, but you're not God."

6. On the Freedom of Choice and Hell:

Contact: "You keep talking about choice."

Christian: "That's right."

Contact: "That's like saying to a starving man, 'If you do what I want, I'll feed you.'"

Christian: "Yes."

Contact: "That's not really free choice."

Christian: "Sure, it's choice. He has a choice."

Contact: "Die, or eat and become enslaved."

Christian: "Wait a minute. Where did slavery come into this? Does society say 'If you want bread, if you want to eat, you'll be my slave'?"

Contact: "That's his choice, either to be a slave or to die. Is that a choice?"

Christian: "Sure, it's a choice. Dying is not the worst thing in the world. Maybe being a slave is worse. You're treating death like it's the worst thing in the world. I'm saying that for some of us, because we know that our destiny is with God in heaven, death is the best thing in the world."

Contact: "At my age, death sometimes looks very good. It's just that I don't like this threat."

Christian: "What threat?"

Contact: "That if I don't believe in Jesus I'm going to go to hell like the rest of the Jews."

Christian: "Like the rest of everybody else, not the rest of the Jews. Like the rest of all people."

Contact: "How do you know that everyone is going to hell? That's a pretty arrogant thing to say."

Christian: "Yes, it is. Why do you think I would say something like that?"

Contact: "You'd probably say it's in the Bible. Am I right?"

Christian: "Where in the Bible would it be?"

Contact: "I don't know. You know, we Jews only

read our Bible—what you call the Old Testament."

Christian: "Have you read it lately?"

Contact: "You're going to tell me Jesus walked around saying that everyone is going to hell. Is that what you're going to tell me?"

Christian: "I can only tell you what the Bible says."

At this point you move the contact into looking at the Bible. You really need to know how to use the Bible in your conversations.

Using the Bible in Conversation

1. A Sample Conversation about Bible Study:

Christian: "Where do you want to study? Where do our differences begin? It's not in the Old Testament part of the Bible. It's in the New Testament part." ("Part" conveys the idea that the entire Bible is equally trustworthy.) "Did you ever read the New Testament?"

Contact: "Never."

Christian: "I could tell. The Bible you have here doesn't have the New Testament. Could you afford to get a whole Bible? One that has an Old Testament and a New Testament?"

Contact: "I have a library card."

Christian: "Good. Go borrow one from the library. Let's get together next Tuesday for lunch. Is Tuesday good for you?"

Contact: "I can't have lunch with you because I play Bingo at 11:00. I could be free at 3:00 for coffee, though."

Christian: "Bingo at 11:00? Is winning at Bingo your priority? I can show you how to win something that is really worthwhile. What good is it to you if you win the whole world and lose your own soul?"

Contact: "Listen. You're a religious person and you may not understand this, but there are a lot of nice friendly people at the Bingo game."

Christian: "Well, maybe I'll get to know some of your friends. Is it all right if I pray with you before I go? I want to pray that God will bless you."

Contact: "Sure."

Christian: "Lord, I thank You for the good health thus far of my friend (name), and that he/she is willing to let me tell him/her what I know about You. Now Lord, I pray that You would give him/her a lift this very day because of his/her openness. Fill him/her with Your joy. In the name of Y'shua, amen."

2. Another Sample Conversation About Bible Study:

Christian: "Last week we were talking about reading the Bible."

Contact: "I'm interested in the Bible."

Christian: "You're interested; that's good. Is that your Bible there? Open it to one of the prophets. Did you ever hear of Isaiah? Open to Isaiah. Find the fifty-ninth chapter. Start reading it. (Always let the person do as much as possible.)

"This prophet Isaiah lived seven hundred years before Jesus. He was a Hebrew prophet. So far as we know, he never left the land of Judea. Now, read me Isaiah fifty-nine."

Contact: "In the Jewish religion we cover our heads when we pray or read from the Tenach. Do I have to cover my head when I read this?"

Christian: "If you want to, or just put your hand on your head."

Contact (after reading): "So the people of Isaiah's time were sinners. God seems to be mad at the people he's talking to."

Christian: "Does He have reason to be mad?"

Contact: "I haven't studied this in a long time."

Christian: "I'll tell you God's complaint against the people of Judea. He brought them into a nice place to live. He said, 'Be nice to one another and do what I tell you. I gave you this country, your bread, your lives. Remember who gave.' Right away they forgot, as though they had created themselves. So God came back and said, 'You're not being nice to each other. Here you are with widows who are not eating and orphans who are going ragged. I gave you plenty, and you won't give to each other.' So God was angry because people weren't doing what He told them to do. They were not behaving the way He told them to behave. Shouldn't He be angry?

"Let me tell you what hell is. Hell is having God hide His face from you because—what does it say there?"

Contact: "Something about iniquities."

Christian: "Now you are getting onto the topic of sin."

3. A Sample Conversation About Sin:

Christian: "What's an iniquity?"

Contact: "I don't know."

Christian: "Do you have a dictionary? I could tell you, but you'd do better if you found it yourself. Even at 87, you're not too old to learn."

Contact: "Iniquity seems to be something like transgression."

Christian: "Or sin, or bothering God."

Contact: "You know what it sounds like to me? If you're saying that people who died in the Holocaust are going to hell and so are a lot of other people, then the Holocaust is no worse an evil than anything else in this world because everyone ends up in the same place anyway. Do you believe that?"

Christian: "Listen, not so long ago/years ago, when I was younger, I was going to hell and I was enjoying myself along the way, but then I found out it didn't have to be that way."

4. A Conversation to Leave the Door Open for Future Communication:

Contact: "I have a lot of questions about the nature of God, the nature of humanity and the nature of evil."

Christian: "Do you know what you need? I can see that you're over here and I'm over there, and excuse me for saying this, but it seems to me that you've already made up your mind about things that you weren't told—like did you know that hell is like having God turn His face from you?"

Contact: "Well. . . ."

Christian: "Did you know that iniquity is sin? Look, I don't have any more time right now, but I'm willing to talk about these things again. I can tell that these things are important to you."

Contact: "I've got a pretty busy schedule, but. . . ."

Christian: "Alright, everyone is busy. I'm busy, you're busy. I'm willing to give you more of my time and I'll come to you. You don't have to come to me. Can you commit to four hour-long sessions? After four hours, we'll see if I learned anything from you, and if you learned anything from me, we'll continue."

APPENDIX II

OLD TESTAMENT REFERENCES
AND THEIR NEW TESTAMENT FULFILLMENTS

Topic	Old Testament	New Testament
Messiah to be of the seed of the woman	Genesis 3:15	Galatians 4:4
Messiah to be of the seed of Abraham	Genesis 12:3; 18:18	Luke 3:34 Matthew 1:2 Acts 3:25 Galatians 3:16
Messiah to be of the tribe of Judah	Genesis 49:10	Luke 3:33 Matthew 1:2
Messiah to be of the seed of Jacob	Numbers 24:17,19	Matthew 1:2 Luke 3:34
Messiah to be of the seed of David	Psalm 132:11 Jeremiah 23:5; 33:15 Isaiah 11:10	Matthew 1:6 Luke 1:32-33 Acts 2:30 Romans 1:3
Messiah to be a prophet like Moses	Deuteronomy 18:15,19	Matthew 21:11 John 6:14 John 1:45 Acts 3:22-23
Messiah to be the Son of God	Psalm 2:7 Proverbs 30:4	Luke 1:32 Matthew 3:17
Messiah to be raised from the dead	Psalm 16:10	Acts 13:35-37
The crucifixion experience	Psalm 22 Psalm 69:21	Matthew 27:34-50 John 19:28-30
Messiah to be betrayed by a friend	Psalm 41:9	John 13:18,21
Messiah ascends to heaven	Psalm 68:18	Luke 24:51 Acts 1:9
Homage and tribute paid to Messiah by great kings	Psalm 72:10,11	Matthew 2:1-11

Topic	Old Testament	New Testament
Messiah to be a priest like Melchizedek	Psalm 110:4	Hebrews 5:5-6
Messiah to be at the right hand of God	Psalm 110:1	Matthew 26:64 Hebrews 1:3
Messiah, the stone which the builders rejected, to become the head cornerstone	Psalm 118:22,23 Isaiah 8:14,15 Isaiah 28:16	Matthew 21:42,43 Acts 4:11 Romans 9:32,33 Ephesians 2:20 1 Peter 2:6-8
Messiah to be born of a virgin	Isaiah 7:14	Matthew 1:18-25 Luke 1:26-35
Galilee to be the first area of Messiah's ministry	Isaiah 9:1-8	Matthew 4:12-16
Messiah will be meek and mild	Isaiah 42:2,3 Isaiah 53:7	Matthew 12:18-20 Matthew 26:62,63
Messiah will minister to the Gentiles	Isaiah 42:1 Isaiah 49:1,8	Matthew 12:21
Messiah will be smitten	Isaiah 50:6	Matthew 26:67 Matthew 27:26,30
The gospel according to Isaiah (The suffering Messiah brings salvation)	Isaiah 52:13-53:12	The four Gospels
The New and Everlasting Covenant	Isaiah 55:3,4 Jeremiah 31:31-33	Matthew 26:28 Mark 14:24 Luke 22:20 Hebrews 8:6-13
Messiah, the Right Arm of God	Isaiah 59:16 Isaiah 53:1	John 12:38
Messiah as Intercessor	Isaiah 59:16	Hebrews 9:15
Two-fold mission of the Messiah	Isaiah 61:1-11	Luke 4:16-21
Messiah will perform miracles	Isaiah 35:5,6	John 11:47 Matthew 11:3-6
Messiah is called "The Lord"	Jeremiah 23:5,6	Acts 2:36

Topic	Old Testament	New Testament
The time of Messiah's coming prophesied	Daniel 9:24-26	Galatians 4:4 Ephesians 1:10
Bethlehem to be the place of Messiah's birth	Micah 5:2	Matthew 2:1 Luke 2:4-6
Messiah will enter the Temple with authority	Malachi 3:1	Matthew 21:12
Messiah will enter Jerusalem on a donkey	Zechariah 9:9	Matthew 21:1-10
Messiah will be pierced	Zechariah 12:10 Psalm 22:16	John 19:34,37
Messiah to be forsaken by His disciples	Zechariah 13:7	Matthew 26:31,56
The coming of the Holy Spirit in the days of the Messiah	Joel 2:28	Acts 2:16-18
Opposition of the nations	Psalm 2:2	Revelation 19:19
Messiah's final victory over death	Isaiah 25:8	1 Corinthians 15:54 Revelation 7:17; 21:4
The glorious Messiah	Isaiah 63:1	Revelation 19:11-16
Messiah as King	Psalm 2:6-9	Revelation 19:15,16
Submission of all nations to Messiah's rule	Isaiah 2:4	Revelation 12:5 Micah 4:1-4
The Gentiles shall seek the Messiah of Israel	Isaiah 11:10	Romans 11:25

RECOMMENDED READING

This list includes some older out-of-print books that contain very helpful information. Most libraries can obtain these older works at your request.

Amber, Lee. Chosen: *Communicating with Jews of All Faiths*. Santa Ana, CA: Vision House Publishers, 1981.

Benach, Henry A. *Go to Learn: A New Approach in Sharing Messiah*. Chattanooga, TN: International Board of Jewish Missions, Inc.

Evangelism Department, Board of Home Missions, Christian Reformed Church. *Jewish Evangelism: Creative Strategies for Churches*. Grand Rapids: Evangelism Department, Board of Home Missions, Christian Reformed Church, n.d.

Gartenhaus, Jacob. *Winning Jews to Christ: A Handbook to Aid Christians in their Approach to the Jews*. Chattanooga, TN: International Board of Jewish Missions, Inc.

Goldberg, Louis. *Our Jewish Friends*. Neptune, NJ: Loizeaux Brothers, 1983.

Fischer, John. *The Olive Tree Connection*. Downers Grove: InterVarsity Press, 1983.

Heintz, Jack. *How to Successfully Win and Disciple Jewish People through the Local Church*. Hollywood, FL: Peace for Israel, Inc., 1976.

Huisjen, Albert. *Talking about Jesus with a Jewish Neighbor: A Keynote in Personal Jewish Evangelism*. Grand Rapids: Baker Book House, 1964.

Kligerman, Aaron Judah. *Sharing Christ with Our Jewish Neighbors*. Cleveland, OH: The Bible House, 1946.

Kolb, Erwin J. *How to Respond to Judaism.* St. Louis: Concordia Publishing House, 1990.

Leaman, James R. *Faith Roots: Learning From and Sharing Witness with Jewish People.* Nappanee, IN: Evangel Press, 1993.

Levitt, Zola. *Some of My Best Friends are Christians.* Glendale, CA: Regal Books, 1978.

Lindberg, Milton B. *Witnessing to Jews: A Handbook of Practical Aids.* Chicago: American Messianic Fellowship, 1948.

Lipson, Eric-Peter E. *Approaching the Jew: The Basis of Understanding.* London: The Wickliffe Press, 1966.

Little, Paul E. *How to Give Away Your Faith.* Downers Grove, IL: Inter-Varsity Press, 1988.

Robinson, Rich. *"Judaism and the Jewish People," Compact Guide to World Religions,* ed. Dean Halverson. Minneapolis: Bethany House, 1996.

Rosen, Moishe. *How to Witness to Jews* (audio cassette set of 2 tapes). San Francisco: Purple Pomegranate Productions.

Rosen, Moishe. *Share the New Life with a Jew.* Chicago: Moody Press, 1976.

Rubin, Barry. *You Bring the Bagels, I'll Bring the Gospel.* Old Tappan, NJ: Chosen Books, 1989.

Ward, Fenton M. *What to Say When They Say, "I'm Jewish": Sharing the Gospel With the Original Messengers.* San Juan Capistrano, CA: Joy Publishing, 1993.

For Witnessing to Russian Jews

Fifth Catalogue of Literature and Resources for Russian Jewish Evangelism. Springfield, VA: Friends of Soviet Jewry, 1997. May be ordered directly at P.O. Box 2567, Springfield, VA 22152-0567.

ANSWERING QUESTIONS AND OBJECTIONS AND BUILDING THE CASE FOR JESUS

Addressed to Jewish Concerns

Chernoff, David. *Yeshua the Messiah*. Havertown, PA: MMI Publishing Co., 1983.

Fruchtenbaum, Arnold G. *Jesus Was a Jew*. Tustin, CA: Ariel Ministries, 1981.

Juster, Daniel C. *Jewishness and Jesus* [booklet]. Downers Grove, IL: InterVarsity Press.

Kac, Arthur. *The Messianic Hope: A Divine Solution for the Human Problem*. Grand Rapids: Baker Book House, 1975.

Kac, Arthur W., ed. *The Messiahship of Jesus: Are Jews Changing Their Attitude toward Jesus?; Revised Edition*. Grand Rapids: Baker Book House, 1986.

Kjaer-Hansen, Kai, ed. *The Death of the Messiah*. Baltimore, MD: Lederer Publications, 1994.

Levitt, Zola. *Jesus—the Jew's Jew*. Carol Stream, IL: Creation House, 1973.

Questions and Answers, compiled by Jews for Jesus. San Francisco: Purple Pomegranate Productions, 1983.

Portnov, Anna, ed. *Awakening: An Anthology of Articles, Essays, Biographies, and Quotations about Jews and Yeshua (Jesus)*. Baltimore, MD: Lederer Publications, 1992.

Riggans, Walter. *Jesus ben Joseph: An Introduction to Jesus the Jew*. MARC; Olive Press; Monarch Publications, 1993.

The Jewish Case for Jesus (audio cassette). San Francisco: Purple Pomegranate Productions.

The Y'shua Challenge: Answers for Those Who Say Jews

Can't Believe in Jesus. San Francisco: Purple Pomegranate Productions, 1993.

Zaretsky, Tuvya. *Turning to God: Good News for God's Chosen People* [booklet]. Downers Grove, IL: InterVarsity Press, 1985.

Messianic Prophecy

Allen, Ronald Barclay. *Lord of Song: the Messiah Revealed in the Psalms.* Portland: Multnomah Press, 1985.

Ankerberg, John; Weldon, John; Kaiser, Walter C., Jr. *The Case for Jesus the Messiah: Incredible Prophecies that Prove God Exists.* Chattanooga: The John Ankerberg Evangelistic Association, 1989.

Baron, David. *The Ancient Scriptures for the Modern Jew.* London: Hebrew Christian Testimony to Israel, no date.

_____. *Rays of Messiah's Glory: Christ in the Old Testament.* Grand Rapids: Zondervan, no date.

_____. *The Servant of Jehovah: The Sufferings of the Messiah and the Glory That Should Follow; An Exposition of Isaiah LIII.* Grand Rapids: Zondervan, 1954, © 1922.

Briggs, Charles A. *Messianic Prophecy: The Prediction of the Fulfillment of Redemption through the Messiah.* Peabody, MA: Hendrickson Publishers, 1988 [orig. ed. 1886].

Clowney, Edmund P. *The Unfolding Mystery: Discovering Christ in the Old Testament.* Phillipsburg, NJ: P & R Publishing, 1988.

Cooper, David L. *The Eternal God Revealing Himself to Suffering Israel and to Lost Humanity.* Los Angeles, CA: Biblical Research Society, 1963, © 1928, 1953.

_____. *Messiah: His Final Call to Israel.* Los Angeles: Biblical Research Society, 1962.

_____. *Messiah: His First Coming Scheduled.* Los Angeles: Biblical Research Society, 1939.

_____. *Messiah: His Glorious Appearance Imminent.* Los Angeles: Biblical Research Society, 1969, © 1961.

_____. *Messiah: His Historical Appearance.* Los Angeles: Biblical Research Society, 1958.

_____. *Messiah: His Nature And Person.* Los Angeles: Biblical Research Society, 1933.

_____. *Messiah: His Redemptive Career.* Los Angeles: Biblical Research Society, 1935.

Culver, Robert D. *The Sufferings and the Glory of the Lord's Righteous Servant.* Moline, IL: Christian Service Foundation, 1958.

Driver, S. R.; Neubauer, A. *The Fifty-Third Chapter of Isaiah According to the Jewish Interpreters.* New York: Ktav, 1970. [Also published as The "Suffering Servant" of Isaiah According to the Jewish Interpreters (New York: Hermon Press,1969)]. Originally published 1877.

Edersheim, Alfred. *Prophecy and History in Relation to the* *Messiah: The Warburton Lectures for 1880-1884.* Grand Rapids: Baker Book House, 1955, © 1901.

Frydland, Rachmiel. *What the Rabbis Know About the Messiah.* Cincinnati: Messianic Literature Outreach, 1993.

Groningen, Gerard Van. *Messianic Revelation in the Old Testament.* Grand Rapids: Baker Book House, 1990.

Hindson, Edward E. *Isaiah's Immanuel: A Sign of His Times or a Sign of the Ages?* Grand Rapids: Baker Book

House, 1978.

Kaiser, Walter C., Jr. *The Messiah in the Old Testament.* Grand Rapids, MI: Zondervan, 1995.

Kligerman, Aaron Judah. *Messianic Prophecy in the Old Testament.* Grand Rapids: Zondervan, 1957.

Levey, Samson H. *The Messiah: An Aramaic Interpretation: The Messianic Exegesis of the Targums.* Cincinnati: Hebrew Union College Jewish Institute of Religion, 1974.

Lindsey, Hal. *The Promise.* Irvine, CA: Harvest House, 1974.

Lockyer, Herbert. *All the Messianic Prophecies of the Bible.* Grand Rapids: Zondervan, 1973.

Meldau, Fred John; Hoglin, Donald A., ed.; Julian, Amy L., ed. *The Prophets Still Speak: Messiah In Both Testaments.* Bellmawr, NJ: The Friends of Israel Gospel Ministry, Inc., 1988, © 1956.

Mills, Sanford C. *A Hebrew Christian Looks at Isaiah Fifty Three.* New York: American Board of Missions to the Jews, 1971.

Patai, Raphael. *The Messiah Texts.* New York: Avon, 1979.

Phillips, O. E. *Exploring the Messianic Psalms.* Dresher, PA: Hebrew Christian Fellowship, 1967.

Reich, Max I. *The Messianic Hope of Israel: Studies in Messianic Prophecy.* Grand Rapids: Eerdmans, 1940.

Riggans, Walter. *Yeshua ben David: Why Do the Jewish People Reject Jesus as Their Messiah?* Crowborough, UK: MARC, 1995.

Rosen, Moishe. *Y'shua—the Jewish Way to Say Jesus.* Chicago: Moody Press, 1982.

Santala, Risto. *The Messiah in the Old Testament in the*

Light of Rabbinical Writings. Jerusalem: Keren Ahvah Meshihit, 1992.

Smith, James E. *What the Bible Teaches about the Promised Messiah.* Nashville: Thomas Nelson, 1993.

Wright, Christopher J. H. *Knowing Jesus through the Old Testament.* Downers Grove, IL: InterVarsity Press, 1995.

Resolving Bible "Contradictions"

Archer, Gleason L. *Encyclopedia of Bible Difficulties.* Grand Rapids: Zondervan, 1982.

Geisler, Norman, and Thomas Howe. *When Critics Ask: A Popular Handbook on Bible Difficulties.* Wheaton, IL: Victor Books, 1992.

General Apologetics

Lewis, C. S. *Mere Christianity.* New York: Phoenix Press, 1987.

McDowell, Josh, and Don Stewart. *Answers to Tough Questions Skeptics Ask About the Christian Faith.* San Bernardino: Here's Life Publishers, Inc., 1980.

McDowell, Josh. *Evidence That Demands a Verdict: Historical Evidence for the Christian Faith.* Nashville, TN: Thomas Nelson, 1993.

McDowell, Josh. *More Than a Carpenter.* New York: Phoenix Press, 1986.

Rosen, Moishe. *The Universe is Broken.* San Francisco: Purple Pomegranate Productions, 1991.

Sproul, R.C. *Choosing My Religion* (Video); Ligonier Ministries.

Specific Issues

Blomberg, Craig L. *The Historical Reliability of the Gospels.* Downers Grove, IL: Inter-Varsity Press, 1987.

Bruce, F. F. *Jesus and Christian Origins Outside the New Testament.* Grand Rapids: Eerdmans, 1974.

Bruce, F. F. *The New Testament Documents: Are They Reliable?* Leicester, England: Inter-Varsity Press; Grand Rapids: Eerdmans, 1985.

Lewis, C. S. *Miracles: A Preliminary Study.* New York: Macmillan, 1978.

Lewis, C. S. *The Problem of Pain.* New York: Collier, 1986.

McDowell, Josh, and Bill Wilson. *He Walked Among Us: Evidence for the Historical Jesus.* Nashville: Thomas Nelson, 1993.

Morison, Frank. *Who Moved the Stone?* Grand Rapids: Zondervan, 1977.

Schaeffer, Francis A. *The God Who Is There: Speaking Historic Christianity into the Twentieth Century.* Downers Grove, IL: InterVarsity Press, 1968.

Sire, James W. *Scripture Twisting: 20 Ways the Cults Misread the Bible.* Downers Grove, IL: InterVarsity Press, 1980.

Sire, James W. *The Universe Next Door: A Basic World View Catalog.* Downers Grove, IL: InterVarsity Press, 1997.

Testimonies of Jewish Believers in Jesus and the Messianic Movement

Cohen, Steve. *Disowned.* San Francisco: Purple Pomegranate Productions, 1995.

Damkani, Jacob. *Why Me?* New Kensington, PA: Whitaker House, 1997.

Dobschiner, Johanna-Ruth. *Chosen to Live.* Palm Springs, CA: Ronald N. Haynes, 1981, © 1969.

Dorsett, Lyle W. *And God Came In: The Extraordinary Story of Joy Davidman; Her Life and Marriage to C. S. Lewis.* New York: Macmillan Publishing Company; London: Collier Macmillan Publishers, 1983.

Einspruch, Henry. *The Man with the Book.* Baltimore, MD: The Lewis and Harriet Lederer Foundation, 1976.

Einspruch, Henry, ed.; Einspruch, Marie, ed. *Would I? Would You?* Baltimore, MD: Lederer Foundation, 1970.

Fieldsend, John. *Messianic Jews.* MARC, Olive Press, Monarch Publications, 1993.

Friedman, Bob. *What's a Nice Jewish Boy Like You Doing in the First Baptist Church?* Glendale, CA: Regal Books, 1972.

Frydland, Rachmiel. *When Being Jewish Was a Crime.* Nashville: Thomas Nelson Publishers, 1978.

Gartenhaus, Jacob. *Famous Hebrew Christians.* Grand Rapids: Baker Book House, 1979.

Gartenhaus, Jacob. *Traitor? a Jew, a Book, a Miracle: An Autobiography; Memorial 1994 Limited Anniversary Edition.* Chattanooga, TN: International Board of Jewish Missions, Inc., [1994, ©] 1980.

Guinness, Michele. *Child of the Covenant: a Jew Completed by Christ.* London: Hodder and Stoughton, 1985.

Harvey, Richard. *But I'm Jewish: a Jew for Jesus Tells His Story.* San Francisco: Purple Pomegranate Productions, 1996.

Hidy, Ross F. *Eddie Spirer: The Little Minister.* San Francisco, CA: Purple Pomegranate Productions; printed in cooperation with the Lutheran History Center of the West and Jews for Jesus, 1995, © 1992.

Katz, Arthur; Buckingham, Jamie. *Ben Israel: The Odyssey of a Modern Jew.* Plainfield, NJ: Logos International, 1970.

Kuschnir, Vera. *Only One Life: A Story of Missionary Resilience; Biography of Leon Rosenberg, the Late Founder and Director of the American European Bethel Mission.* Broken Arrow, OK: Slavic Christian Publishing, 1996.

Levitt, Ken; Rosen, Ceil. *Kidnapped for my Faith.* Van Nuys, CA: Bible Voice, Inc.,1978.

Levitt, Zola. *Confessions of a Contemporary Jew: The Story of a 20th-Century Levite.* Wheaton: Tyndale House Publishers, Inc., 1975.

Marcus, Warren M. Shalom: *One Man's Search for Peace; A Filmmaker's Autobiography.* Nashville, TN: Thomas Nelson, 1993.

Rosen, Moishe. *Jews for Jesus.* Old Tappan, NJ: Fleming H. Revell, 1974.

Rosen, Ruth, ed. *Jewish Doctors Meet the Great Physician.* San Francisco: Purple Pomegranate Productions, 1997.

_____. *Testimonies.* San Francisco: Purple Pomegranate Productions, 1987.

Roth, Sid; Harrell, Irene. *There Must Be Something More! The Spiritual Rebirth of a Jew.* Brunswick, GA: Messianic Vision Press, 1994.

Schlamm, Vera; Friedman, Bob. *Pursued.* Glendale, CA: Regal Books, 1972.

Telchin, Stan. *Betrayed!* Lincoln, VA: Chosen Books, 1981.

Zeidman, Alex. *Good and Faithful Servant: The Biography of Morris Zeidman.* Burlington, Ontario: Crown Publications, 1990.

Jewish Believers and the Jewish Holidays

Buksbazen, Victor. *The Gospel in the Feasts of Israel.* Philadelphia: The Friends of Israel Missionary and Relief Society, Inc., 1954.

Glaser, Mitch; Glaser, Zhava. *The Fall Feasts of Israel.* Chicago: Moody Press, 1987.

Lipis, Joan R. *Celebrate Passover Haggadah: A Christian Presentation of the Traditional Jewish Festival.* San Francisco: Purple Pomegranate Productions, 1993.

Lipson, Eric-Peter. *Passover Haggadah: A Messianic Celebration.* San Francisco: JFJ Publishing, 1986.

A Messianic Look at Christmas and Hanukkah. San Francisco: Purple Pomegranate Productions, 1995.

Rosen, Ceil and Moishe. *Christ in the Passover.* Chicago: Moody Press, 1978.

Zimmerman, Martha. *Celebrate the Feasts of the Old Testament in Your Own Home or Church.* Minneapolis: Bethany Fellowship, 1981.

Messianic Interest

Brickner, David N. *Mishpochah Matters: Speaking Frankly to God's Family.* San Francisco, CA: Purple Pomegranate Publications, 1996.

Brown, Michael L. *Our Hands are Stained with Blood: The Tragic Story of the "Church" and the Jewish People.* Shippensburg, PA: Destiny Image Publishers, 1992.

Cohn, Leopold, ed.; Cohn, J. Hoffman, ed. *The Chosen People Question Box.* Brooklyn: American Board of Missions to the Jews, Inc., 1945.

Crombie, Kelvin. *For the Love of Zion: Christian Witness and the Restoration of Israel.* London: Hodder & Stoughton, 1991.

Edersheim, Alfred. *The Life and Times of Jesus the Messiah*. Peabody, MA: Hendrickson, 1993.

_____. *Sketches of Jewish Social Life; Updated Edition*. Peabody, MA: Hendrickson Publishers, 1994.

_____. *The Temple, its Ministry and Services; Updated Edition*. Peabody, MA: Hendrickson Publishers, 1994.

Einspruch, Henry, ed. *Raisins and Almonds*. Baltimore, MD: The Lewis and Harriet Lederer Foundation, 1967.

Einspruch, Henry, ed.; Einspruch, Marie, ed. *The Ox...the Ass...the Oyster...* Baltimore, MD: The Lewis and Harriet Lederer Foundation, 1975.

Einspruch, M. G., ed. *A Way in the Wilderness*. Baltimore, MD: The Lewis and Harriet Lederer Foundation, 1981.

Fruchtenbaum, Arnold G. *Hebrew Christianity: Its Theology, History and Philosophy*. Tustin, CA: Ariel Minstries, 1983.

Heydt, Henry J. *The Chosen People Question Box II*. Englewood Cliffs: American Board of Missions to the Jews, 1976.

Jocz, Jakob. *The Jewish People and Jesus Christ*. Grand Rapids, MI: Baker Book House, 1979.

_____. *The Jewish People and Jesus Christ after Auschwitz: A Study in the Controversy between Church and Synagogue*. Grand Rapids: Baker Book House, 1981.

Kac, Arthur W. *The Spiritual Dilemma of the Jewish People: Its Cause and Cure;* Second Edition. Grand Rapids: Baker Book House, 1983, © 1963.

Kjaer-Hansen, Kai. *Joseph Rabinowitz, 1837-1899: the Herzl of the Messianic Jewish Movement*. Grand Rapids: Eerdmans, 1991.

Motyer, Steve. *Israel in the Plan of God: Light on Today's Debate.* Leicester, England: InterVarsity Press, 1989.

Riggans, Walter. *The Covenant with the Jews: What's So Unique about the Jewish People?* Tunbridge, Wells: Monarch Publications, 1992.

Schiffman, Michael. *Return of the Remnant: The Rebirth of Messianic Judaism.* Baltimore, MD: Lederer Publications, 1992.

Telchin, Stan. *Abandoned: What is God's Will for the Jewish People and the Church?* Grand Rapids: Chosen Books, 1997.

Jews and Judaism
Basic Jewish Beliefs (non-Christian)

Donin, Hayim Halevy. *To be a Jew: A Guide to Jewish Observance in Contemporary Life.* New York: Basic Books, 1991.

Kolatch, Alfred. *The Jewish Book of Why.* Middle Village, NY: Jonathan David Publishers, Inc., 1981.

Kolatch, Alfred. *The Second Jewish Book of Why.* Middle Village, NY: Jonathan David Publishers, Inc., 1981.

Steinberg, Milton. *Basic Judaism.* Northvale, NJ: Jason Aronson, 1987.

Wouk, Herman. *This Is My God: The Jewish Way of Life.* Boston: Little, Brown and Co., 1988.

Jewish History

Ben-Sasson, Haim H. *A History of the Jewish People.* Harvard University Press, 1976.

Johnson, Paul. *The History of the Jews.* New York: Harper & Row, 1987.

Sachar, Howard M. *The Course of Modern Jewish History.* New York: Vintage Books, 1990.

Resources for Follow-up and Discipleship

Growth Book: Especially for New Believers. San Francisco: Purple Pomegranate Productions, 1994.

Maas, Eleizer and Fran Anderson. *Stand Firm: A Survival Guide for the New Jewish Believer.* Lansing, IL: American Messianic Fellowship, 1990.

If you would like more help in witnessing
to your unsaved Jewish friends, contact:
Jews f✡r Jesus
60 Haight Street
San Francisco, CA 94102-5895
E-mail: jfj@jewsforjesus.org
www.jewsforjesus.org